Toxic Forgiveness

Beatríz Pelayo-García, Esq.

Copyright

Copyright © 2021 by Beatríz Pelayo-García, Esq.

All rights reserved. No part of this book may be reproduced,
stored in a retrieval system or transmitted,
in any form or by any means,
without the prior written consent of the publisher or a
license from Digi-Rights Direct LLC. For a copyright license,
visit http://www.copyrightsnow.net/ or call toll free to
copysupport@digi-rights.com

Cataloguing in publication information
is available from Library and Archives U.S.
ISBN 978-1-956257-02-1

Pierucci Publishing
www.Pieruccipublishing.com

Edited by Jonathan Grant
Jacket design by Stephanie Pierucci at Pierucci Publishing
Interior design by Stephanie Pierucci
Printed and Bound by Amazon.com

Dedication

Joshua and Conrad, my Kings, you are the very reason I was put on this earth, to be your Mom. It has been a long journey and perhaps not easy, but however it was, whatever it cost, I would change nothing to simply have this opportunity to be your Mom. I love you both so big!

To my mother and father, Beatriz Garcia Pelayo and Esteban Pelayo, thank you for always holding space for me. The way you love your children and grandchildren is the highest calling of love. To all my siblings, Luis, Elizabeth, Bob, and Maribel, thank you for supporting me always. My aunt, Rose Mary Garcia, not all children are born of the womb, some are of the heart. I am yours because your heart is huge! To my chosen family, the Ceja family, thank you for always holding space in my life and being my greatest cheerleaders.

Connie Villafan, my sister from another mister, in all my darkness, you have been the light. Esther Gardiner, you move mountains to create magic because you say so. To all the staff at Distinguished Legal Group, prior, current, and future, you are the change in this world, one case and one heart at a time. Yvette Villafan, under your guidance, we have affected the lives of so many because every case is an opportunity to change a life and no one embodies that more than you.

Debra and Michael Bernoff, you will never know the effect you have had in my life. You are the game changers and source of living my best life. Wendy Amara, thank you for your amazing coaching that forwarded me in my life. Elizabeth Yang, you are the best buddy in the world! Your very being inspires and brings out the best in me. Dwight Anthony Schmidt, II, my beloved Yin Yang twin, nobody loves more than you and for the stand you take for others, I acknowledge you and love you. To the amazing trainers that have crossed my path to propel me forward, Kathy Benson, Chris Lee, Michael Strasner, Rodrigo Garcia Platas, Mary Jo Lorei, Nichole O'Brien, Bettie Spruill, Matt Pinto, Sue Keith, and Sylvia Badasci, from the bottom of my heart, thank you for your humble servant leadership. Dr. Leslie Anne Ross, thank you for always bringing me back to my heart because that is where my strength lives.

Finally, I acknowledge the legend of Margo Majdi, Mastery in Transformational Training. Although we have never met, you have changed my life. Perhaps the greatest legacy of all is the effect you have when your body is no longer present on this earth. If that is the key to living your best life, challenge accepted! This world is a better place because you said so. And here I am!

Thank you all for what, up until now, is the most courageous moment in my life. I am humbled to be in the presence of great leaders. Thank you, again.

Table of Contents

Copyright 2
Dedication 3
Dear Reader 7
Prologue 9
Part I 13
Growing Up 13
At Your Service 21
Dan 27
The Man at the Hotel 35
Charm and Deaf Ears 45
Star-Crossed 55
Power 61
The Switch 69
Without Breath 77
Numb 85
Shame 89
Enough 97
Part II 107
Escaped 107
Masculine and Feminine 113
The Absolute Illogic 117
Moving Forward 121
Love and Goodnight Hugs 127
King Days and Fat Suits and Self-Work 133

Reconnecting 141
Touch Therapy 147
High Times 155
The King of King Days 161
Part III 169
Manifesting 169
Gene Keys and Gibran and Gods and Goddesses 177
Unexpected Life Lesson 187
Why Victims Don't Get Help 189
Stories From my Ministry 201
Nuggets from my Ten Love Letters Lesson 211
A Brief Review—and Father's Day 221
Anger or Forgiveness? 227
Fear, and Overcoming It 233
On Forgiveness 239
Life is Good 245

Dear Reader,

This book will take you on a journey deep into the prison that one woman experienced during three years of captivity by an abusive partner.

Among stories that will bring you both laughter and tears, you will learn how this woman was brutally beaten, how her children were used as leverage, and how she barely made it out alive, even after her escape, through self-harm perpetuated by shame, disassociation, and trauma.

As you're reading this book, understand that these stories may trigger past traumas in your own life and body.

You may feel compelled to share this book with somebody you suspect may be trapped in an abusive relationship. And if you, yourself, are in an abusive relationship, please know that you are not alone.

As this book inspires you, we encourage you to find a trusted counselor, psychiatrist, life-coach, or pastor with whom you can share the emotions that may arise during your reading.

Beatríz is neither a licensed psychologist nor doctor, and her stories are designed solely to share one woman's journey while inspiring others to find safety from toxic abuse.

If you are seeking legal or emotional support for your own journey and healing from abuse—or to help somebody you love—please visit www.beatrizpelayogarcia.com/course/ where you will find a vault of videos Beatríz has created to share more behind-the-scenes details of her own escape.

In this comprehensive Toxic Forgiveness masterclass, you will learn:

- Why Victims Struggle to Escape

- How Beatríz Escaped Her Abuse

- How to Forgive Yourself and Your Abuser

- How to Return to a Life of Love After Abuse

Visit www.beatrizpelayogarcia.com/course/ for your special access to this education and to experience your own LIVE Recorded Masterclass with Beatríz.

If you are looking for legal assistance or representation in your own separation, escape, or divorce journey, please email Beatríz at Support@DistinguishedLegal.com

Your Escape Plan is coming,

Team Beatríz

Prologue

I am 47 years old, which means I've lived 44 years of freedom. Not a bad ratio, but for those three years in my early 30's, I lived in bondage. In fear. In a prison with bars forged of my relationship to myself and the relationship to a man. A man who abused me. A man who punched me and stabbed me and suffocated me and called me every name you could think of and more.

And he did these things all the time.

For the past thirteen years, I have been unable to speak to this man. After I finally ended it, finally got out, finally escaped, I tried to talk to him once, just to see if I could. I could not.

The image of him telling me, repeatedly, how he'd kill me and kill the kids and then go down in his 'blaze of glory' is far too etched in my mind.

That was the card he would play—that if I ever tried to leave, he'd kill me and then kill my sons and then kill himself. Murder-suicide, all of us bleeding-out and dying slow and agonizing deaths at his hands.

And you know what? For a long time, I could've cared less if he killed me. Actually, a lot of me wanted him to kill me. So I could finally be free.

But "I'll kill the kids" was all I ever heard.

I was trapped, in hell.

*

But I finally got out of that hell. I finally made an escape plan and followed through on it. I finally accepted the help of those who loved me. I finally stopped living for mere survival and started living to live.

This book was a long time coming. I wasn't sure if I had the strength to tell my story. I wasn't sure I wasn't still afraid to do so. But the butterfly afraid of changing remains in the cocoon, never to fly. I've been flying for a while now—as a mother, in my profession, in my personal and social life—and I want to help others do the same.

If you are in an abusive relationship, this book was written for you. If you know someone in an abusive relationship, this book was written for you. If you've ever abused someone, this book was written for you. And if you happen to be one of the lucky few who has managed to live in this world and never heard of the realities of abuse, this book was written for you.

This book is the story of a human being written for human beings. None of us has it easy in this life. But all of us can, from this point forward, make the decisions that lead us to a better one.

This book is my story. This book is my humanity. This book is my message. And this book is for you.

Thank you,

Beatríz

Part I
Growing Up

"But we were not lack for opportunity. And that word, especially for the children of immigrants, is a golden word."

You'd think I came from a broken family. You'd think I'd been abused as a little girl. Hit. Shamed. Cigarette burns or something. I wasn't. Nope. I grew up with love. I grew up loved. Hugs and kisses. Birthday parties. I grew up with good parents who treated me like parents should treat their daughter.

My parents are still happily married to this day, ready to celebrate their 50th wedding anniversary, still holding hands and giggling together. My mother is my rock and my father is one of the kindest, most gentle souls you could ever meet. It doesn't make sense that I ended up in the abusive relationship I got myself into. I had, by all accounts, a good childhood.

Maybe it was too easy? Maybe I lacked adventure or adrenaline-pumping action or drama and subconsciously sought it out with the men I became interested in? Maybe. I just don't know. Neither do the therapists. It's a tough one to pin down.

*

When my parents came to the United States as immigrants, their intention was to get married, buy a house, stay for a while, then sell it and return to Mexico. Well, needless to say, their plans changed. When they decided to stay and raise their children in the United States, they decided that education would become the number one tool for their kids.

All five of their children are college graduates. That is the most atypical of statistics for the children of Latino immigrants. (And four of the five of us have at least one graduate degree.) They told us that "you are either a leader or a follower." Based on results, we have all become leaders.

My brother is a professor of mathematics, and we all do dynamic work in dynamic fields. Because of our devotion to education.

We got this from our folks. From their love and empowerment and from how much value they put on school. On some level, we could even get out of housework by doing schoolwork. I would finish my homework and didn't necessarily like mopping and taking out the trash, so I started getting extra library books. There were always these contests at school on who could read the most books, so my dad would take my sister and I to the library where we would each get our own grocery bag of books. I would read every word of every book from my bag and then start in on the books in my sister's bag. I read a lot. I became a voracious learner.

I think my parents caught on, but how could they be upset at their girl for wanting to read? I suppose they let me slide on the mopping.

It was about the only thing they let me slide on. Because they were immigrants and they wanted us to have more than they had.

We were poor, at the level of poverty where we had just enough to realize all that we did not have. I used to hate Christmas because my dad would often get laid off just before the holidays—not his fault, he worked in the garment industry cutting the patterns for the seamstresses and that was just the way they operated. But, because of it, there wasn't ever much under any tree for me to rip open.

But we were not lack for opportunity. And that word, especially for the children of immigrants, is a golden word. My parents got us into private parochial schools through grit; they convinced the schools to give us a lot of help to do so, and we got a family discount. But there were a lot of wealthy kids at that school, and it became obvious all of the things they had that we did not.

As I got older, I became the student body president of my high school and then the student body president of my college. This position in college afforded me a weekend retreat to a ritzy golf club in Southern California with the board of trustees.

These people had crazy amounts of money. That weekend I saw checks being written for multiple hundreds of thousands of dollars. It was a new world for me. To see the plushness, the glamour, the money, the lifestyle and how these people acted. It was an eye-opening couple of days in my life.

One morning I got to talking with the wife of one of the trustees. She was fascinated by me, by my background and my ethnicity, by how I didn't look like really anyone else there. It was almost like she was on safari talking to a member of the Kalahari.

"Did you grow up with any money?" she asked me.

I thought it an odd question, but I answered politely and straightforwardly. "We had a house, but not much else. I only had a couple changes of clothes. Our sandwiches were bread, mustard, lettuce, cheese—and it was government cheese."

"Ooh—what's government cheese?"

"You really don't want to know. Doesn't taste very good."

"Sounds like you didn't have much."

"My dad had a blue-collar job. We were the kids of immigrants, and we knew it."

"How did you cope? I mean, a woman needs to feel secure..."

I could tell she meant that a woman needs to feel secure financially, that a woman needs to be taken care of in monetary ways. Her husband had ambled over to the conversation, and I now asked her a question: "Do you think money is a factor in your marriage?"

She got tongue-tied. She didn't know what to say and didn't say much. I did. "My dad may not have given me a lot of money," I said, "but he gave me love and he gave me support and he gave me everything I need."

"Oh," she said, blank faced, feigning a look to the watch on her wrist. "Hmm, you know what? I have to leave—our tee time is coming up..."

I felt like I had learned that trustee's wife a thing or two.

Shortly after that weekend, I recounted the story to my parents. I could see the smile of pride on their faces. It made me feel good to stand up for how I was raised, to stand up for my immigrant parents and what an amazing job they did raising me.

Though they were proud of me a lot during my childhood, there was only one other time in my youth where I saw that same look of pride on their faces—after I won the area spelling bee in 8th grade. I had earned the right to represent my school against all the other parochial schools around. I was the only Latina competing, the only representative of my people amongst a sea of white faces.

And I won the whole thing.

So we got to go to Burger King. We loved to go to Burger King, but still we kids were only allowed to choose our type of hamburger. No French fries or soda. My mom would bring our own sodas from home—and the government cheese.

"But mom! Cheeseburgers taste so good because the cheese is melted!"

She wasn't having it. I got my hamburger and she put a slice of government cheese on it, and we proceeded to enjoy our family outing to the restaurant.

As we were eating, this Latino man came up to us, came up to me. "You're the girl who won the spelling bee, right?"

"Yes, I am."

He looked at me, sighed, and smiled. "We spoke about you at our dinner table that night," he said. "Thank you for representing our people."

And the look on my father's face was worth more than a million dollars would ever be. Tee time at the club or no tee time at the club.

At Your Service

"Your best life

is possible

because you say so."

Before we get into the heavy stuff, before we enter the crux of this story, I have to tell one last little story from childhood. One little story from Beatríz the little girl. Because, at the core of me, the crux of me, is that little girl.

Before the spelling bee and before the class presidentships and before law school and before being an attorney and before being an abusee and before writing this book, I was a preschooler. Most likely like you were. And I was innocent, most likely like you were. Life hadn't hurt me yet. I was open to the world, learning new things every hour of every day, most often with a smile upon my face.

The story is this: I am three and a half years old. The colored pictures and graphs are upon the wall and the building blocks are over in the corner and our little desks are empty because our teacher has us in a circle on the floor. We are all sitting cross-legged.

We are about to do an activity, and it involves something I have never seen before. Rice Krispy Treats. My people didn't do Krispy Treats, and they were new to me. Who am I kidding—the only cereal we had was generic corn flakes. I don't think I even knew what Rice Krispies were. All rice I knew was accompanied by beans. This was so brand new! I saw them, saw them being cut into squares and pulled apart, all that gooey goodness, and I think to myself I gotta get in on this as soon as possible!

To get one, to get our own perfect little square of Krispy Treat, we had to say our complete name aloud to the group. Then we had to say our mom's complete name aloud to the group and our dad's complete name aloud to the group. We could say it in English or Spanish; I guess I went with a sort of Spanglish.

My turn came. I wanted that Krispy Treat. "My name is Beatríz Alicia Pelayo-García, *a sus órdenes*."

A little giggle came from one of the girls, but I didn't think much of it. All I could think about was that magical-looking square of crisp and goo. So I quickly said, "My mom's name is Beatríz García Pelayo, *a sus órdenes*."

More giggles—a few of my classmates laughed at that one. My teacher hushed them up a bit and asked me, "And what is your dad's name?"

"Esteban Pelayo Villaseñor, *a sus órdenes*."

The classroom burst into laughter.

See, '*a sus órdenes*' means 'at your service.' It is a common way to say your name in some Latino households, and especially in mine. "Beatríz Alicia Pelayo-García, at your service," was what I was saying. Because I thought that was my name. To me, at that age, that was my name.

I remember not understanding why everyone was laughing. I shrugged it off and got my Krispy Treat and enjoyed learning of a new wonder of the world.

Years passed. Classrooms changed. More lessons were learned. Still, I had no idea why I made my classmates laugh that day.

It wasn't until I was eight or nine that I realized what I'd done, how I said my name back in preschool believing *'a sus órdenes'* was simply part of my name.

I mean, we Latinos do have long names, but *a sus órdenes* is not on my birth certificate.

Taken in one lens, I think this anecdote did show my teacher that I was raised to mind my manners. That I had good, (firm) parents, and that we had respect for rules in my home.

Through a broader lens, the tale may serve to show that those words really were, and are, a part of my name—that I live my life as a life of service. Of service to others.

In service is how I run my firm. It is how I talk with the abuse victims I work with in my courses outside of my firm. It is how I live my life. In service.

And as we turn the page from preschool to adulthood and begin to get into some stuff that gets pretty heavy, *a sus órdenes* is how I will endeavor to do it—going to some dark places only so we may see the light that shines on the other side.

Dan

"Forgiveness is the only thing that help the victim "make sense" of the abuse."

I liked boys growing up. I did. In high school, I dated a couple guys. I bought the dress and got my hair done and went to prom. I was always super focused on school, on my grades and on my future, so boys didn't become an obsession for me like some other girls. But, yeah, I liked boys and as I grew up, I liked men. I liked being complimented. I liked the attention. I liked being told that I was beautiful.

I made it through high school and through that prom and got into a good college. It was there that I met Dan. I met him when I was a twenty-year-old flower and we dated through college and law school, up until I was ready to take my first big law school exam at age twenty-five.

Dan was a drug addict.

Needless to say, it was not the best relationship a girl could have, but I guess I didn't know that. He was my first serious boyfriend, and I suppose we accept the love we think we deserve.

Again, with what a loving relationship my parents showed to me, I'm not sure why, or how, I ended up with Dan. Yeah, I liked that he was a poet and how he wrote his heart out. Although he had a rough past—at fourteen he found his brother after he'd shot off his face, an event that caused his mother to die "of a broken heart"— Dan was brilliant in his own way. And he had a good heart. Of course, he was handsome, and there was just something about the way he looked at me that made me feel so special. Sure, he'd "do his stuff," but at the end of the day I thought it was a good relationship.

It was not.

Dan was mean. He'd demean me and put me down. He would make me feel small and then build me back up again. He was the addict, but maybe I was addicted to the behavior. Five years with this guy? I know, I know.

I was going to college while working more than full time, because I was working multiple jobs. I was also the president of my sorority, and I supported us as he lived with me in the sorority house where he would try to hide his crack addiction. Drastic ups and downs were par for the course. He would be fun and charming and then nasty and suicidal. In an instant. He would try to hide his pipes, but I would find them, and when I did, I'd put them out in plain view for him to see. Yeah, I was sending a message, and it was: "I know what you're doing."

The logical part of me thought that 'if he knew that I knew', then he would stop. Well, no, that's not how that happened. He would deny it. In fact, he was so committed to the lie that he had us going to therapy, having me believe that it was a mental health issue.

He threatened suicide all the time, and I would talk him down. "No baby, no..." Maybe it made me feel important. Maybe it made me feel needed. Again, I'm not sure. I've spent over $80,000 at therapy in my life, and I am still not sure.

Usually, I felt his suicidal threats were some sort of act he was putting on. Some cry out for help, some cry out for attention. But one time they felt pretty real. And it involved me. We were in the car, Dan driving, and I was in the passenger seat. We were coming home from being out somewhere, can't for the life of me remember where. We were going over my favorite bridge, a beautiful span in Pasadena known as the Colorado Street Bridge—but it's also gained the unfortunate moniker of 'Suicide Bridge.'

It was night and the bridge lights made me smile as I saw them approaching. We came up to the bridge. Dan had a bad idea.

"I'm going to drive us off this thing!" he screamed, and there was something in his voice that made me believe he was going to do it.

"No, Dan," I said. "No, you're not!"

We argued. I begged him not to. I let him know that he had so much to live for. He got more upset. The more that I spoke, the more upset he became. I didn't know what to do. So, I prayed. I prayed to God and begged for another chance.

At my wits end, I made a promise. "God, if you let me live, I will leave him."

Dan didn't drive us off that bridge into a watery grave. But he did drive me to seeing that it probably wasn't the best relationship, that this probably wasn't the man to be with. And I had made a promise to God. So I left him.

Was it easy? No. Did it hurt? Yes.

It hurt for so many reasons. A deep part of me that believed I was his last reason to live, that he was alive only because I was there. Was this coming from ego? No—I didn't want that responsibility, it just felt like it had landed square upon my shoulders.

So, yeah, in the moment it was difficult to leave Dan. It is crystal clear now, but it wasn't back then. Not with how I saw the world. Not with how I saw myself.

See, I'm a smart girl. A smart person. It feels weird to say that, but I am. My IQ scores are pretty darn high. I could go on and on about doing well in school, to the extent that my placement after my first year of law school (where you are ranked according to grades) earned me a scholarship to continue the rest of my education at minimal costs, about how I graduated with honors and was the Editor-in-Chief of the International and Comparative Law Review, about how I am a successful attorney.

But some things, it seems, take me a long time to learn.

The bridge incident finally led me to break it off with Dan.

Until, regretfully, I let him back in.

He called me up, out of the blue one day. "I'm sober," he told me. "And I'm doing well at work."

I believed him. Too easily. I agreed to go out with him and we had a good time.

A few mornings later my younger sister phoned and frantically woke me up. She told me how she'd had a dream, a nightmare: "I saw you, you were excelling, doing great in law school, living life, but then you got back with Dan and everything went down the drain for you. You lost it all…"

The color drained from my face. I had to sit back down because I felt like I was going to faint.

You see, no one knew that I had seen Dan. Not my sister. Not my mom. No one.

And I was reminded of my promise, my promise to God: "If you let me live, I will leave him."

So, once again, I ended it. I had to. And this time more firmly. Door shut, nothing ajar. I thought it would be the last I would hear from him.

It wasn't.

A little over a year later, he called me again. On the night before my Civil Procedure final exam. (In law school, your final exam is usually the entirety of your grade. The entire semester or year rides or dies on these exams.) I needed to focus and prepare. He insisted on speaking to me.

I redirected him, saying, "If you need help, you should speak to our youth group leaders, or your family or friends," or basically anyone but me because I needed to be 100% focused on my exam. He begged me to speak with me. He told me he needed me. He told me he loved me. He told me that I was the only reason he was still alive.

I told him that I was open to having this conversation another day, but that I could not do it now.

We had that conversation, and I held firm on my promise to God. I told him I couldn't do it anymore, that it was over.

His sweet talk turned anger-filled, and with harsh words he told me if I didn't give him another chance that I'd never see him again.

A few weeks later, he was dead. Dan was gone. He got back heavy into the drugs and his heart had stopped. He was right, I would never see him again. I didn't hear the news right away, and when I did, I was about to board a plane to China for an International Law course.

It was a long flight. I had a lot to process. I was beyond sad that he was no longer on this earth, yes, but I was proud of choosing myself, for not going down that road with him.

I had escaped just in time.

I was able to do this at that time in my life. I didn't know, then, how difficult it would be to do in the future.

Dan had pushed his body too hard, gone too far. I wish I'd known that I had already gone too far with this type of relationship.

I had not.

The Man at the Hotel

"Every day you stay

is a choice

to remain."

I aced that first exam in Law School and then aced the next two. I'd graduated from my accelerated night program near the top of my class, while working 40+ hours a week to support myself and pay all expenses not covered by my scholarship. No small chore, but the end was near. The only obstacle that stood in the way of me becoming the attorney I'd always dreamed of being was the Bar.

And that test, the Bar, is a pretty tall bar—not nearly everyone who graduates law school ever passes the thing. There are very intelligent and dynamic law school graduates in this world working in other fields, not by choice, but because they did not pass this one test.

So, we study our tails off for it. Most prospective takers generally enroll in one preparatory course to get ready for the Bar Exam. Not good enough for me. Four felt right to me. Yep, not one—not two, not three—four. I'd always been an overachiever and don't like leaving things in my professional life to chance. Who needs sleep, right? What's a few extra thousand dollars? I was about to be making lawyer money.

So I signed up for four courses to ensure I passed the Bar on the first try. I would not be like Joe Pesci in My Cousin Vinny failing this thing multiple times—I wouldn't be middle-aged before I passed this exam. (And I wouldn't ever wear a leather jacket to court either.)

There are multiple aspects to the California Bar Exam, which is a combination of essays, performance tests, and multiple-choice questions. So I chose to study for it the only way I knew how: comprehensibly.

I even took another course that was for 'repeat test takers,' even though I was a first-time taker. I was committed, and I was clear that I would pass. I would be ready as the wind to take and ace this thing because I was only going to do it once.

The last course I chose to enroll in was held in San Diego because I had a class to attend, I believe, all days except two during the time I was studying for the Bar. Since it was a multiple day course, it was too far to drive. The commute from Los Angeles to San Diego just wasn't going to work. It was a two-hour drive each way if the traffic was good—which, let's face it, it was Southern California, so it never was.

"I'm wasting too much time on the road," I told my mom. "I'm just going to get a hotel down in San Diego."

I wish I hadn't. I wonder if my life would have been different if I'd just stayed with the commuting and come back to my parent's house to sleep each night.

But I made that hotel reservation.

I drove down 'The 5', got through the traffic, made a couple lefts and rights and pulled up to the hotel. It wasn't the most expensive place, but it wasn't a dive either. I dropped my car off at the valet and walked through the sliding doors into the lobby, past the soft black leather chairs and the television set streaming the news, and over to the front desk.

And there he was. This good-looking guy with a cashmere smile.

"Checking in?" he said, his eyes a gorgeous shade of hazel.

He was charming, right off. He really was. From behind the counter, he smiled, and my heart melted. He was so sweet and kind. He had strong facial features. He was handsome. He had a presence.

He made some comment about us "beautiful women making his day amazing" and it made me laugh. He gave me and a girl friend of mine advice on where to go in the city and what to do—which places had the best Taco Tuesday and where to get the best margaritas, things like that, and he just smooth-talked the crap out of us. He even got us some amazing Italian food delivered to us in the hotel for a great deal through a discount he had. And, with everything, he was so friendly, so smooth.

"He's cute, right?" I asked my friend up in our room later that night.

"He is."

The next day I woke up early and went to my class. I came in with great focus and studied hard. It was a long class and that evening I found myself back in the hotel, in the lobby, and I just sort of drifted over to the front desk as if on a whim. I said, "hello" and we started talking again, almost like old friends or something. He was funny. He was charming. He had a way about him.

"You want to grab a drink?" he asked, that smile and those eyes.

I'd been a ball of stress. The courses were demanding, and the test was not too far away. I needed a break from it, and a handsome man had just asked me out. Why not?

"Sure," I said, almost giddy.

We went out to one of the oldest bars in San Diego, Tivoli's, right there in the Gas Lamp District, and we had a good time. It felt comfortable, natural. The conversation came easy. He was a talker, and I let him talk. He told me stories, and he made me laugh. I drank my drink and forgot about the law for a couple hours.

It felt good. Being around him made me feel good. Since the Bar exam was coming up, I came back to finish the last few days of intense studying, but I immensely enjoyed the distraction.

*

Then it came. The Bar. The test that would determine my fate. I would fail or I would pass. I would become an attorney, or I would not.

The air was tense. Everyone was stressed out. It's a three-day exam, mind you, and people were on edge. I could tell that caffeine and other (more revved-up) stimulants were being ingested at high levels. I could feel the energies of my cohorts: so tight, so locked in, so hyper focused.

But me? I actually felt pretty light. Maybe for the first and last time in a long time.

I had prepared more and better than everyone else who was in the room with me. I knew this, I felt this. I was ready. It was time to show up and show off.

I'd been grooming myself for so long for this thing that I felt like I should almost enjoy it. It was like a football player making the Super Bowl; I was there, had been working my whole life to get into this room; I should take pride in this fact, revel in knowing that I had done everything I could possibly do to put myself in the best situation to do well.

Plus, I knew I was going to ace it.

The sessions were long, meant to be grueling, but I was feeling good. There wasn't a question I didn't know the answer to. Words were flowing out of me like water down a stream, and I knew I was doing it. I could see the pained look on cohorts around me, could feel their lack of breathing, but I was floating.

On our breaks between sessions, I'd call Ryan. (We'd hung out a few more times and exchanged numbers.) I would push the button on my phone and it would start to ring and then he'd answer.

"Hey pretty lady, how's it goin'?"

"Oh, hey! I'm so ready for this thing, I'm having fun with it."

"Nice!"

"Yeah, I'm actually pretty energized."

And we'd just chat and keep it light and enjoy a fun little conversation. It was like we were in high school or something, getting our five minutes on the phone in between study breaks. I'd look around and see—almost feel—the stress of other test-takers around me, and it was like I had this secret that no one else had. I had someone to talk to. I had a friend to make me laugh, and they did not.

It felt good. He, Ryan, was making me feel good.

On day three, I finished the exam and called him right up. "I did it!" I screamed like a little girl.

"Yeah, you did! Grab a drink?"

"You bet."

*

Everything in my career had led to this point. I'd been battling for so many years, through high school and college and law school—working jobs the whole way through—just for the opportunity to take the Bar. I'd just taken it, and I knew I'd passed with flying colors. I had to wait a while for the results, but I knew I was going to become an attorney. I knew my dream was coming true.

When I walked it felt like my feet weren't even touching the ground. And Ryan was there to dote on me—to flatter me and to hold my hand and to kiss my neck and to whisper sweet words into my ear.

It should have been a little fling. He should have been my 'Bar Exam Boyfriend.' Maybe a month of drinks and dates and sex. Maybe even a one-night stand. I initially came to San Diego for one night. I ended up staying for two weeks.

I should have limited it to what it was. I didn't.

I checked out of the hotel and told him I would call him. I drove back up the 5 to L.A., back to my parent's house where I lived. It was hard. It didn't feel right. Yeah, I loved them a ton, but I was 29 years old with career and freedom on my mind. I needed to spread my wings, to take flight—and living with my folks became too much.

Talking on the phone with Ryan only made me want to see him more. He was so dang charming. So complimentary. So funny and cool. I drove to San Diego often.

We'd hang out and go to the beach, go to museums, get drinks, or just walk around the city holding hands. He brought out the fun side of me. He brought out joy and passion, romance, things I hadn't felt in years. I'd been so focused on my career that I hadn't allowed myself these things in so long. I hadn't allowed myself to feel. I'd been so in my head that I had forgotten about my heart. For the past four years, I'd been working from 8-5 only to get off and head into law school by night. Then I would eat, sleep, and repeat. I had become a machine. I see now that turning into a machine made me lose some of my human-ness. Some of my humanity. I had worked myself—my brain, my body, my soul—to its limits. With all the work, with all my time going to the pursuit of a singular goal, I really think I lost my mind.

I had become a blank slate. And Ryan was there to imprint upon it.

Charm and Deaf Ears

"Choose yourself

and

choose life."

We were different people, Ryan and I. I suppose every couple can say that, but with us it was like we were from two different worlds. I liked dancing. He liked going to bars. I liked reading. He liked talking to people. I had just become a practicing attorney. He worked in the service industry.

That last one didn't bother me, though. He was holding down three jobs—two restaurant gigs and the front desk position. It was impressive. He worked hard: six, seven days a week, and I saw it. I saw him working. I saw him earning. It didn't bother me that he didn't have a degree past high school. In all honesty, it didn't.

I don't know if he, though, could have said the same about my education.

"Damn college motherfuckers!" he'd say. The first time I heard it was at some comment made by a person near us at a restaurant.

I let it pass, let the comment slide. I perked my eye at it, sure, but I didn't say anything. Maybe he'd had a bad run in with some academic-types at work that day?

I gave him the benefit of the doubt.

When I heard that comment a second time—"damn college motherfuckers!"—I should have said something. When it became a near-daily mantra, said with a certain vehemence behind it, a personal tone of anger and real spite, I should have noted it as a red flag. The first red flag. But I did not.

He would snap out a "college motherfucker!" here and there, but then snap right back into his charming, funny, complimentary self. I was falling in love with him, falling in love with this man, and my blinders were already up. Anything that didn't fit my image of the man and who I thought he was, who I wanted him to be, was shut out. And those compliments, the flattery, the treating me like the princess I'd always wanted to be treated like—not like mean drug-addict Dan—well, they further dampened those blinders over my eyes.

Ryan, for me at this time in my life, was Tom Cruise on the couch on Oprah spouting to the world, "I AM IN LOVE WITH KATIE HOLMES!!!"

He was literally that overt, that over-the-top about his affection for me. I'm talking about the man I'm dating (me, my man!) getting down on his knees and looking me in the soul through my eyes and giving me roses. Like, weekly.

I'm talking about the man I'm dating shouting out to the entire bar, at octaves that made people stop and look, "I Love this Woman!! I love Beatríz Pelayo-García!!"

I'm talking about the man I'm dating, the man I'd only just met a few weeks prior, showing me complete adoration. Me—a girl who'd only read about this kind of treatment in romance novels or seen in fairy tales. Ryan made me feel like a queen. He really did.

He complimented me, he flattered me, he wined and dined and swooned and crooned me. He showed me exactly what I wanted to see, and I ate it up by the spoonful. And it dulled my senses. It numbed my wits. It made me blind.

*

Even early on in our relationship, when things were still like that rose in bloom, my parents didn't like him. They never came to me and said it flat out, but it was clear through the tone of their voice and the language of their body that he was not their favorite, that they really did not approve of me being with him.

"Well," my mom might hint, "he is ten years older than you…"

"Yeah," I'd come back. "He's a man. I like that about him."

"And, he doesn't have much of an education," dad may chime in.

"He works seven days a week! You don't need to have a college education if you have an amazing work ethic."

They would shrug, and I would go on thinking Ryan was the one the proverbial stars had lined up for me.

Around October, three months after we met that first night at the hotel, I was back down in San Diego, again, having driven down the 5, again. (He hadn't driven once to L.A. to see me, not once. Blinders?)

We were out to dinner. He was doting on me something good. The hand holding, the neck nibbling, the complete attention of my man placed squarely on me.

He looked me in the eye, a big wide wonderous smile: "We should move in together."

I held his gaze and took a moment. "So soon?"

"I know we should," he said. "I have this feeling and I know it—I should move in with you."

"Really?"

"Yeah, you already have your practice set up in L.A., and there are so many serving jobs up there that it'll be easy for me to get one—heck, three or four."

I was smitten, and the man I was slowly beginning to think may be the one for me had just made his intent clear. He wanted to take the next step. I did too. "Okay," I said, and we kissed and we hugged and I thought about our dream future together.

"But since I've never taken a vacation," he put in, almost as an aside, some sort of afterthought, "I think I'll come up and take like two weeks off before I start the ole' job search."

"Yeah, sure," I said, blinders on firm. "That sounds fun. That sounds good."

A few days after that conversation, Ryan stopped his lease in San Diego and moved in with me. Onto my lease at my new place in L.A. He took his two-week vacation and things were golden-hued. We walked the beach and sipped cocktails. We made love and laughed.

But, after those two weeks were up, the job-search never commenced. The two-week vacation extended. And extended. And then extended some more.

It was about this time that I should have started to pay attention to those *señales de alarma*—those things known in English known as red flags.

The first was "college motherfuckers!"—how he said it and what I was coming to think he meant by it, like he felt cheated, betrayed or something. Like he felt he was above the hand he'd been dealt. Like there might be some disconnect between the reality betwixt Ryan's ears and the reality of what was actually happening. The second was the extension of his vacation.

I didn't heed them. The only flags I saw were ones that were pronouncing "to death do we part."

"I'm making great money," I'd tell my friends when they hinted about his not working, about his not paying rent. "He's just taking some time to relax—to recharge."

Then there was this, something he said almost under his breath when he was talking about future plans for us: "I left my second marriage because I was getting too angry."

Hmm. Yeah, he'd been married twice before. Don't think I mentioned that. And to leave the second one because of anger? Yes, I should've taken more note of that one.

Little tidbits and truths of his previous life would drip out like an old faucet that sometimes leaked dirty water. I learned that his first marriage ended with Ryan doing time. Yep—it had gotten physical, and he had to pay the price in jail.

Also, when he was in the Navy, at one point coming out-of-harbor, he was put in the brig for assaulting a Japanese woman.

"It was all bogus," Ryan explained away after he let the story slip, doing his best to cover his tracks with rose-petals of lies. But I couldn't help myself from thinking: to be put in the brig meant his own officers and peers had seen the reality of the situation differently than Ryan had…

When living in Nevada earlier in his life, he'd received a "disturbing the peace" for a domestic altercation. *Señal de alarma.*

And more than a few members of his family had cut him out of their life. *Señal de alarma.*

But, as Ryan told it and I tried to believe, they "were assholes" and he was glad to be rid of them.

But there was one thing I had real trouble getting over: Ryan's own mother had cut him out of his life. Yeah, big *señal de alarma*, right? She'd shunned her own son, preventing him from speaking to her "until he got help."

Help with what? Again, the blinders kept the red flags from being seen.

I even got a letter in the mail from one of his uncles: "Beatríz," it read, "be careful with Ryan. He may have some kind of condition…"

When someone's own family wants nothing to do with the person you have found yourself with—even if he seems like the perfect guy who's come along at just the perfect time—it is a sign. One that should be heeded. I did not.

And I got in deeper. A lot deeper.

Star-Crossed

"Forgiveness can be false power, false strength."

I met Ryan in August of 2004. By November of that year, I was pregnant.

We hadn't used contraception. As a Catholic, that was a pretty big deal for me; if I ever got pregnant, there was really no going back. I was not on the pill and he told me often how much he disliked condoms. He also—more than once, multiple times, repeatedly, almost incessantly—told me he was sterile.

"I am," he told me. "From being near the nukes on the ships."

"Seriously?"

"I'm 40 years old. I've been married twice. No kids. I think I shoot blanks."

In hindsight, it's impossible to say for certain whether he thought he was telling the truth, whether in his mind he really thought he was sterile—or if he was intentionally lying, slinging mistruths like torpedoes to get me as committed as possible as fast as possible. Whatever his motivation, Ryan proved as capable—if not more so—to give the sperm to inseminate the ova as any man out there.

We had sex. We didn't use contraception. The stork came. Just like they told me it would back when I was younger.

What I didn't learn when I was younger was that I would find out all on my own. No 'being late,' no trip to the drug store to buy the test that revealed the two pink lines. Nope, for me, I just knew. One night I just felt it, felt that I was pregnant—some ancient motherly instinct kicking in to tell me I'd just done my job as a biological entity and created life.

Even though I knew I was with child, knew beyond all doubt that my man was, in fact, not sterile, to prove it to Ryan I went to the drug store and picked up a pregnancy-test kit. I brought it home and went into the bathroom and did what the instructions told me to do and came out into the living room.

"Babe, I have something to show you."

I opened my palm to reveal the two little pink lines that would change both of our lives forever.

Ryan, who was what we call in Spanish a *labioso*— literally 'a lot of lips,' a talker, a rambler, a jokester, a wooer, a schmoozer, a yap-yap—fell silent. His eyes went as wide as two full moons.

"So this is what it takes to shut you up?" I said, smiling, happy, so dang happy.

And he laughed, and we laughed together, and we cried and hugged and smiled.

Then Ryan started talking again. "We have to tell people. We have to tell everyone!"

I was hesitant to do so. "Maybe we should make it through the first trimester?"

"Nonsense. We tell people now. We celebrate this gift. We tell people, now."

Ryan had said it, and so we did it. We told everyone we knew. Well, more like he told everyone we knew. He told our friends. He told my coworkers. He told people we met on the street. He—Ryan, not me—told my parents. About their daughter's pregnancy. About my pregnancy.

But nobody he told showed elation at the news. No one was happy for us or for the baby to come. Well, maybe the strangers on the street who didn't know us, who didn't know him, were okay with it; but everyone who was familiar with our relationship was not excited that we were going to bring a child into this world. Sure, they'd say the right things but you could tell the feeling wasn't there. "Oh, that's... great," they would say with a nod and a smile forced through near-gritted teeth, maybe a nod and an awkward hug. "I'm so happy for you, that's so good."

While no one went out and said the word 'abortion' (especially not in my house), I could almost feel the urging through the words they actually spoke. I pushed it away. I pushed away anything that was not 'pro Ryan,' pushed it out of my reach, away from my senses. We'd only been dating for four months, and the bloom was still on the rose. It was butterflies and roses and champagne and sunset-walks on the beach.

Honeymooned-tones of happiness and wow.

One night, I walked outside our apartment and looked up into a deep winter's sky, the stars shining so bright they looked like they were dancing in shimmering gowns. I'm 30 years old. I've passed the Bar. I'm a practicing attorney in Los Angeles. I've found my man. I'm pregnant with my first child.

I looked up to those bright shining stars. "The universe has aligned," I said aloud. *"Todo está perfecto."*

I looked up to the stars and didn't know how star-crossed I was.

Power

"...for how bad things got, there was almost this equal and opposite bliss in the beginning..."

I was living. I was working. I was pregnant. And I began to notice the red flags peeking out.

"How's the job search going, Ryan?"

"Ah, don't worry about that," he'd say, staring at the television from his cemented spot amid the living room couch. "I'm going to stay home and take care of the kid."

"Well—"

"—You're working so much, Bea, our child will need one of us around. Don't worry, I'll do it."

And he'd flip through the channels and tune me out and that was, well, that. It wasn't 1950 anymore, I told myself, and I'm not going to stop working. It's not the worst idea to have a parent at home for the formative years—no childcare, no nannies... yeah, why not?

I'd win the bread and Ryan would be the stay-at-home father.

He was already nearly six months into that two-week vacation. In theory, he'd been applying for work. At least, that's what he told me. He was always "searching the internet, filling out applications," but I never saw it. All I heard were the excuses: "They say I'm too old, that damn restaurant's only looking for 20-somethings—and the other one I told you about hired some illegal!"

I don't know if he ever planned to work. I still don't know. But, through one lens it does seem easy to say that he may have had a plan, one executed perfectly: Find a lawyer. Knock her up. Live on the couch. Get fed. Have some sex. Get a kid or two out of it. Do what I want.

The only problem was that he needed someone to play the role of the 'working wife-mom' in that plan, and he happened to find me. Or maybe I unconsciously signed up for the gig? I'll never really know. I've blamed myself about 5,482,329 times. I've blamed Ryan almost as many.

I blamed God and the universe and those stars I talked to that one night too.

Yes, children can be used as pawns. Children can be made to hold us hostage. It's an interesting thing to identify. I'm pretty sure that's how Ryan saw it with me. Because it wasn't long into the pregnancy that all those *señales de alarma* I keep talking about added up to a big fat red mark on my life.

But before I go into that, into the first time he hit me, the first assault, I have to show you some of the things that drew me to Ryan. Some of the powers he had. Because, for how bad things got, there was almost this equal and opposite bliss in the beginning. It was so good. So fun. So passionate. He had this power.

He was so in tune with me. Yeah, I think I'll start there—with how uncannily 'in tune' the man named Ryan could be.

As the pregnancy advanced—from that first night I 'just knew' until I delivered our baby—I never, not once, had morning sickness. Ryan did. Never did I wake up in the wee hours and go pray to the porcelain goddess. Never did I experience a single symptom other than a growing belly. Not once did I have to miss work because I was not feeling well or in pain. My man did. For me.

Ryan, somehow, absorbed my symptoms and took them upon himself. He sucked them up like Michael Clarke Duncan in The Green Mile, sucked out the sickness from me like you would if your partner got stung by a rattlesnake out in the wildlands of Utah. Suck it up and take it on and then spit it out.

Ryan did that. I still don't know how. But he did. He got sick. For me.

"Bea," my law partner told me one day at work when I was about four-months, "sometimes I forget you're even pregnant. You never complain—about anything."

I explained why.

"Wait—Ryan gets morning sickness?" he asked me in clarification, disbelief thick on his tongue.

"Yep. And I don't."

My man was taking on all my symptoms, absorbing my pain so I could be the best for our child. And I was having so much fun being the new attorney in town that I obviously wanted to keep working; in the moment, it felt like he was allowing me to do it, allowing me to keep being me. It felt good. Great. It felt almost heaven-sent.

That was the first time I thought that Ryan—the *labioso*, the man who could talk and talk, spin a yarn and make you believe it like Rasputin or something—may have some actual, tangible powers.

Stick with me here. I'm not crazy. Well, maybe I am a little crazy, but I do, even today, think there is some validity to the fact that Ryan had—was endowed with—some special, almost supernatural abilities.

"It's a boy," he told me one evening early in my pregnancy. "I can feel it. I can see it." His eyes were distant as he spoke, almost prophet-like, a seer looking into the sands of time. "I've always had this vision... even when it didn't happen with my first two wives—I've always had the vision of a son, Joshua Alexander. That's his name. And I can see his face and I can hear him laugh. And he is my son. Joshua Alexander."

I could feel the energy coming off Ryan as he spoke. It was otherworldly, like something from the Oracle at Delphi, like the word of God in the Bible.

"I'm a Scorpio, Beatríz," he told me another time. "I'm a dragon—and I was born in 1964, the Year of the Dragon. So I'm a double dragon. And I've had visions... my whole life I've seen myself with a tiger, a double tiger, just like you."

I'm a Leo, born in 1974, the Year of the Tiger.

"We complete each other," he went on, his eyes traveling from that place of distance right into mine: personal, intimate, powerful. "We complete each other. It is meant to be."

Even in just the way he talked, the way he could talk and talk and keep people listening, keep them hanging onto whatever might come out next—reality or make-believe or something in between—he was transfixing. He was magnetic. Not unlike the cult leaders we've seen on the news or read about in the papers, he would say things and people would believe them. Not everyone, but many.

I know I did.

"I am an angel," he would tell me, and even the first time I heard the words coming out of his mouth I knew he absolutely believed what he was saying. His belief, that unwavering belief in the words that came out of his mouth—even if you knew he was telling half-truths or all-out yarns—he'd make you believe. And not just me either. He'd obviously been married twice, had made at least two other women believe. And who knows how many other romances and flings he'd had?

"I am an angel," he'd repeat, and I'd half-think my Ryan just might be.

But the Good Book tells us that angels have fallen. The scripture tells of archangels and demons. And they have powers too. There are workers of light and there are people and powers drawn from the dark realms.

I am drawn from the realms of light.

I grew up in a religious world. A very Catholic world—and like most religions, our stories asked us to suspend reality in order to believe them. They ask us to escape the world we know and live in to travel back in time to a more primal place, a more raw place, a place where the boundaries between living and dead were blurred, a place where light and dark mingled and did battle, were doing battle, where spirits and magic still dwelled, where exorcisms still took place, a world where certain people—it was known—had certain, special qualities called 'gifts.'

I'd felt my pregnancy the moment my egg had been fertilized—the moment that life commenced its symbiotic growth with my womb. IQ tests and other cognitive-ability scores in my life had shown almost unmeasurably in their scope. But Ryan, the man I met and instantly knew, the man who absorbed my pain and I believed was an angel, seemed even more powerful than me.

A match made in heaven that descended into the abysses of the darkest hell.

The Switch

"Inside my mind,

I said, 'I'm not above

forgiveness.'

Those were my last words

before captivity."

I'm pregnant. Three months in. We're at a bar. He's drinking. I'm not. We're talking to different people. Small talk, etc., just having an evening out.

At some point, I'm talking to a woman, and he starts to get really jealous. He'd had more than a few drinks. I'm getting a little annoyed; I'm pregnant and tired and if you're not part of the party, you get over it.

Ryan ordered a shot. And then it just stayed there; he wasn't drinking it, and I was ready to go home. "Are you going to drink that?" I asked.

And he gave me this crazy-eyed look. A look I'd never seen before. A look I did not recognize.

It scared me. Very badly.

I wanted to leave. I had the keys to the car in my purse, so I walked out of the bar. He followed. "Gimme the keys."

I just wanted to go home, to be home. "You've been drinking. Just let me drive."

"We only live two miles away!"

"Exactly, let me drive."

We must have been getting loud because a crowd started forming outside the bar. People were watching. People were listening.

"Just give me the keys!"

"No!"

And right after I told him 'no,' he did it. He reared back and popped me right in the face. His fist, my cheekbone. He hit me hard.

"Oh my god!" the crowd erupted. "Somebody call 9-1-1!"

He ran. Ryan saw that what he'd done had been seen, and he ran—around the corner and he was gone.

The crowd pointed and made sounds as he ran away.

My urge to get out of there was heaven-high. I opened the car door and turned the ignition. I drove home in fright, in panic. My face was throbbing and my mind was running. I parked in the driveway and kept the motor running. I ran into the house, picked up my dog and hopped back in the car and started driving.

"This will all be over soon," I kept telling myself as I was driving. "This will all blow over."

But, still, I took DandeeLion with me. That look I saw in his eyes, that red craziness, told me I didn't know what this person was capable of. That I didn't know who this person was. If I didn't take DandeeLion with me, I feared for her safety. I didn't know where to go, so I parked myself at the police station parking lot while I was figuring it out. I didn't know how long to stay away or where to go or what to do—I was going to figure it out. I just needed a minute—

My mom called me. "What happened?"

"How do you know?"

"Ryan called me. He told me some things."

Ryan had phoned my mom and called me every name under the sun. "Bitch," he called me. "Whore," he called me. To my mother. He called me a "lesbian" because I was talking to a woman at the bar. He blamed the whole incident on me. To my own mother, he had framed the thing, him hitting me in the face, as my fault.

"Where are you?" my mom demanded.

"In the car."

"Come home, Beanny. Come here, now."

So I drove to my mom's house and slept there. I'd taken Ryan's set of keys when I picked up DandeeLion because I knew if he found them, he'd start driving around looking for me and maybe kill himself or someone else.

I slept uneasily that night. On again off again. Nervous. Images from the night flashing in my mind's eye.

He called my mom again in the morning. "I'm sober now—can I have the keys."

"Okay," my mom said, fighting against her instinct, and we drove them over together.

And what do we find? Do we find a remorseful man, an apologetic human being on his knees praying to be taken back? No. We find a house torn apart. We find destruction. We find anything and everything of value of mine in the house broken. Shattered. Anything with a name brand on it—Prada, Louis Vuitton—soiled, stained beyond repair with bleach poured all over them. All makeup, destroyed. Lamps and art and furniture in pieces, destroyed. The front lawn littered with my things, the front lawn looking like a tornado-swept yard-sale of broken dreams.

So, did I leave right then and there like I should have? Like most people would? No. Did I feel strong, put my foot down, draw a line in the sand? No. I felt humiliated. Weak and humiliated. That's how I felt.

I tried to talk it out with Ryan, subconsciously wanting him to reassure me, my mom hanging back to let us be adults. "Where do we go from here?" I asked him.

He was argumentative. Then he was apologetic. Then he turned on that charm. He told me what I wanted to hear and I chose to believe him. That was a mistake.

So was this: I turned to my mom. "You can go. I'm staying."

"You're what?!"

I saw it as a one-time thing. I saw it as a blip. I rubbed my belly. I thought of my child. I'm not above forgiveness, I told myself.

Forgiveness is one thing. Toxic forgiveness is another.

This wasn't just going to be a blip; this wasn't going to be "just this once." Deep down, I knew that—and even if I hadn't known that, in this one night, this one incident, he'd punched my face as hard as he could and destroyed years of what I had attained. My things, my stuff, my identity. That one time should have been enough to walk away.

*

They say that forgiveness is a universal concept, that regardless of our religion, of our creed, forgiveness is human. That's how I was raised, at least it's what I internalized. Forgiveness was something that wise, good people did.

Ryan loved me and he was the father of the child growing inside me, and so this had to be an aberration. "Nothing but a bad night," I consoled myself, "could've happened to anybody. I will not be the one to throw the first stone."

Well, obvious to say that the first stone had already been thrown. And I hadn't flung it. Ryan had thrown a whole battalion of stones.

The blinders were on good, and I forgave, toxically.

This ill-fated forgiveness, I see now, gave me a sense of power. False power for sure, false strength, but it gave me the feeling like I was above the situation, like forgiving—letting go—gave me some level of control in this otherwise crazy, fucked up situation.

The mind will do some crazy things to keep the mind sane. By choosing to forgive, my mind was able to move itself from victimhood to a position of regaining a sense of power. It made me feel elevated—above Ryan's disregard, above my mother's urging me to leave him, above my own better judgements.

So I forgave, and I tried to forget.

If I could just go back to that moment knowing what I know now—seeing what I see in this stage of my life that I blinded myself from back then—yeah, I would have left. I would have filed a restraining order and left. I would have raised my child on my own, without that man. I would have.

Yet, still, I don't know if I would have changed the forgiveness part. I think I would have forgiven, because that's who I am; but I would have put up boundaries. I would have forgiven healthily, keeping my self-respect, and getting out while still forgiving the human being.

I could have forgiven the human being and still not given him a second chance. It took a lot of therapy and transformational trainings to be able to say those words, but that's what I would have done.

Without Breath

"From the time,

I showed him that he could

treat me like dirt and get away

with it;

I became something upon

which to be trod."

The rest of the pregnancy was a blur. After that first instance of abuse, that supposed 'onetime thing,' it never stopped. From the time, I showed Ryan that he could treat me like dirt and get away with it. I became something upon which to be trod. Walked on. Beaten. To return to for more.

I remember starting to live with my breath held. I was constantly tense, never at ease. I never knew what was going to trigger him next. It could be the smallest things—a comment, the weather, the way someone looked at him on the street. I could never place the logic of what made him tick.

It could be something as simple as him watching Law and Order on television and seeing the attorneys talking to one another. Out would come the, "you college mother fuckers!" and I knew the fuse had been lit. It was only a matter of time before the bomb went off.

He said that line at least three times in one week when we were watching T.V: "College motherfuckers..."

I couldn't take the inanity of it. "You know you can just change the channel," I said.

He looked at me like I'd just told him the world was going to end. "Don't—do not tell me what to do!" he foamed. "Do not, Beatríz, or else."

Ryan switched on me. The honeymoon was over, the bloom having wilted and fallen off the rose. He'd carried on his act as long as he could, and the true nature of the man was coming forth like a waterfall. Gone was Tom Cruise on Oprah, replaced by Tom Cruise locking Katie in the tower. Only, I'm pretty sure Tom never threatened to kill her.

Sure, I'd still see glimpses of the man I fell in love with, glimpses of that guy behind the front desk who wooed me blind. Glimpses of the act—and it was those glimpses that kept me around, those breadcrumbs back to the fairytale he'd leave along the path. But more and more, that version of Ryan was fading. More and more, that Ryan from the hotel was coming to seem like the act, not the real thing. That version was being buried beneath the monster I was getting to know.

But, still, he would come and go, change from day to day.

When Joshua was born, Ryan was beyond excited. He became almost manic, and, for a time, the abuse slowed. There were actually a few weeks in a row when I was not struck by him, when I wasn't thrown down the stairs or otherwise threatened.

Maybe he's cured? I thought, I hoped, I told myself.

The adoration returned to his eyes. I hadn't seen a crazy look in him for a while. He'd look at Joshua and be so enthralled, so loving. I couldn't believe it. He had become a father, and he really did show love for that boy. I thought it changed him. I thought he was cured, that I was saved. When looking at that time—when looking at the polaroid of that moment rather than the whole movie of our relationship—I can say that Ryan was a good dad.

Or at least he was really good at putting on a show.

And then the show ended, and the nightmare started up again. He beat me. He beat me again for the first time in weeks. Then again about a couple weeks later. Then, well then, the intervals got shorter.

About five months after Joshua was born, he got frustrated, angry. "All I'm doing is changing diapers," he screamed at me one night as I was returning home from the office, "and you get to out into the world!"

"Someone has to make money."

And then that crazy look appeared, the extremely scary one, the one I hadn't seen since before I gave birth to his son. From then on, the moment I got home from work, he'd hand the child over to me. Often with no words at all, his straight-elbowed hand-off of our boy saying, "It's your child. I've been with it all day. Do your job and leave me be."

About a month later, some continuing education classes I'd signed up for commenced. They were on the weekends, and that did not go over well. "Oh, great—now I don't get my two days off this week!"

Two days off? I never got two days off.

I walked into the kitchen and pulled the calendar off the wall. I held it in front of him. "I work from here to here"—indicating Monday through Friday with my finger—"making money so we can have this home, and the moment I walk through that door you hand all responsibility to me. I've had the kid every single weekend he's been alive. I work all day and am the parent all night and every weekend—except this one, when I'll be working. So, when are my days off?"

That set him off. I knew it would, but I had to be heard. He beat me good that night.

Ryan was usually pretty creative when he beat me. Whether it was getting me naked and making me kneel on beans he'd spilt on the kitchen floor and berating me with abusive words; whether it was putting his lighter in my mouth and threatening to spark the flame; whether it was stabbing me, with a knife or scissors or anything else he could find, fourteen separate times. Fourteen. I never kept a running tally or anything, but one day I counted up all the different scars.

Some are healing. Some won't ever go away. And, in a very real sense, none of them will ever go away.

Often, he'd grab a knife and go straight for my vagina. I have the stab marks on my inner, upper thighs to prove it.

I've thought about this a lot. Thought about men and women and penises and vaginas. About female genital-mutilation throughout the world, throughout history. I've never come to anything definitive on why men do it, or why Ryan did it to me, but there must be something deep-seated in some male's minds to hurt women where we are most feminine. I've spoken with other women on the subject. I'll probably keep thinking about it my entire life.

*

I never knew which Ryan I was going to get. That 'living with my breath held' kept up. It got worse. When he was getting upset, when that fuse was burning down and the rage was building up, he'd literally make it impossible for me to escape—he'd take my wallet, my keys, even my shoes, and hide them.

He never tied my feet together, but he literally made it so I could not leave the house. And even if I managed to do so, he made it so I wouldn't have been able to get very far.

The stabbing wasn't even the deadliest thing he did to me. Yeah, I could have bled out from the wounds, sure. Probably was closer than I thought a couple times. But it was weird, after he'd stab me, he'd flip a switch and then come take care of me, come take care of the wound. Find some gauze and take care of the bleeding. Like a mouse playing with the rat before he kills it.

One time—no knives involved—I knew he was close to killing me. I was close to death, could feel the life-force draining as I slipped over to the other side. He was suffocating me with a pillow. It was so scary, so scary to be completely unable to breath, to feel your body's mechanisms slowing down and preparing to shut off.

That night didn't start with the suffocation. No, first he came at me with the belt. I ran from him, throughout our house, out one room and into the next. He was bigger than me, stronger for sure and, ultimately, faster. He tackled me to the ground and must have reached for whatever was closest. A pillow from off the couch. I saw him reach for it—and as he threatened to descend it over my face, I saw his eyes. They'd gone black. Completely and utterly black.

He was possessed. "Who are you?" I screamed, and then my final words before he almost murdered me: "What is your name?"

He did not say 'Ryan.' He said a completely different name, from a voice beyond, something guttural and detached, a demonic voice that uttered a demonic name.

And then he shoved that pillow onto my face and pushed down with all his weight. As my life was draining from me, second after second without breath, every moment closer to death, I had this thought—this flash in my mind that came and went in an instant.

As I was being killed, my mind produced a soothing image: If he kills me, I'll be dead. I'll be dead and he'll be in jail. And my parents will have my kids. And everything will be okay.

Numb

"Finally,

it became easy to forgive

because

I became detached."

I became so used to the pain. So inured to it. Physical pain, at that time, was just something I became numb to. I was in such physical pain, every day, that the actual experience of pain almost wasn't there anymore.

But I couldn't show this to Ryan. I couldn't show that he was no longer hurting me physically because I truly believed he was beating me to see me show pain. That is how I felt and that is how I still feel. He would beat me until I yelled or shouted or screamed. He would beat me until it was evident that he had caused me pain. He would beat me until he got the satisfaction of my screams.

So I would give him the show. Even after the beatings stopped hurting, I would yell and scream. If I didn't yell in pain, or mock pain, the beatings would have proceeded. And even though I couldn't necessarily feel the pain, I knew the damage he was doing to my body. And I knew a body could only take so much.

The few times I didn't react, he got even more angry, more amped up, more violent. It was only after I would yell or scream that he would yell his own "shut up!" and the beatings would stop.

But, after a while, I truly did not feel the pain.

The only thing that manifested as anything like physical pain was the growing inability to sleep on my back. For some reason, that's where much of the trauma went. Other than learning to sleep on my stomach or my side, I had become numb.

But the numbness only went toward the physical pain. The emotional pain never really went away. I lived with it constantly. And it was only growing, only getting more painful. I was not well. I was not healthy. I knew I needed to leave, but I had not yet figured out when or how I would do it.

Shame

*"No one will judge

you harder than

you're judging yourself..."*

I survived that night. I survived being suffocated by a pillow being shoved hard and deep onto my nose and mouth, cutting off the airflow to my brain and body. I survived not being able to breathe. I survived Ryan. For one more night.

At this point, I can almost feel you saying, "Why did you not just leave this man?"

I could make excuses. I could talk about Joshua. I could talk about how I wasn't strong enough. But the truth is, I was just not ready. I know that answer will not satisfy you. It does not satisfy me now, but it was my truth in that moment.

And don't get mad at me here, but it wasn't too long after that last incident I described that I actually had sex with this man.

I know.

But for me, sex was a way to take back some of the control of the relationship, a way to placate the man, a way to get his energy out and avoid the fight. It was a tool I came to use to avoid getting beaten. (Or at least to elongate the periods between the beatings.)

Women tell me all the time, "How could you possibly have intercourse with that man after he nearly killed you!" My answers, unfortunately, just aren't that good.

He'd snap out of the demonic state and snap back into the charmer. And I was hooked, hooked by the things he said (never looking at the things he did), and how I always thought it could get better. That it would, for some reason, get better.

So we had some sex. It seemed to make him less apt to hurt me. But when you have sex there are things that can happen. One thing in particular.

And, yes, I got pregnant again. I became pregnant and, once again, Ryan absorbed the morning sickness. He once again told me how he was "an angel," told me—and showed me—his special powers.

Some days and weeks were okay. I remember even laughing a little. But then the monster, never too far away, would return. When I was nine months pregnant, Ryan pushed me down the stairs. I tumbled and rolled and hit my head. I was bleeding, instantly bruised. I thought he was trying to kill me again. I thought he was trying to kill me and the baby inside of me. I landed at the bottom of the stairs, struggled to my feet and looked up at him. I gave a look of defiance that somehow halted him. My keys were still in my pocket. I ran out the front door and jumped into my car.

I screeched out of the driveway and drove, just drove. I had the thought that I should go to a casino—these things are open 24 hours, I won't look weird here. So I did. I sped over there and parked in the big parking lot and went inside where I wandered around the maze of blinking lights and buzzing sounds. I sat down at a slot machine and just looked at it with a thousand-yard stare.

I didn't know what to do. I knew I was not at fault, knew it was Ryan who pushed me down the stairs, but the shame was back. Looking back now, I can't believe how I felt ashamed to get pushed down a flight of stairs with a nine-month fetus inside of me. I should have felt angry. But, what I felt, was shame.

And, after a few hours at the casino, I got into the car and drove back home. I drove right back to the man who'd just pushed me down a flight of stairs.

*

I never opened up to my mom. Not about anything of Ryan or our relationship. The first time she saw me after the staircase incident, she saw my bruises. They were pretty obvious, pretty overt. I saw the look in her eye, and it said a lot. "What happened to your arm?" she asked.

"Oh that? I fell."

"You fall a lot, don't you?"

I could hear what she was actually saying; I wasn't that out of tune. And I knew she wanted to say more but that she knew that I wouldn't have accepted it.

As long as she didn't know I was getting stabbed, I told myself, she'd leave me be. Let me be an adult and make my own decisions. As long as she didn't know I was getting suffocated to death or thrown down the stairs, she'd leave me to manage my own life—but mom definitely knew something bigger was going on than I was letting on.

The thing is, though, abuse is not unlike an addiction; until you're ready to admit that there is a problem, abusees will defend the abuser just like the addict defends their use. We will. It's crazy, I know. And if someone, my mom for instance, would have pushed too far, I'd simply have cut her off. I'd have shut her out, wouldn't have come around to say hello anymore.

My mother, somehow, innately, she knew this.

She was smarter than I knew. She knew she'd have to play her cards perfectly in order for me to open up, in order for me to see what was going on. She didn't want to lose me so she never pushed too hard. The only thing that a parent or a friend can do when someone is mired in an abusive relationship is to say, in their own words, "you have a safe place to come when you are ready."

That's what my mom did for me. She kept me close until I was ready to put my foot down and do what needed to be done.

*

At this point, my life was day-to-day. Day-by-day. I was living to survive. I wasn't looking to the future or to the past. I was simply trying to stay alive. And, because of this—this constant state of flight-or-flight—I didn't attach to my children the same way most mother's do.

I'll expand more upon this later.

Our second son was born, and I knew, subconsciously, that the only way I'd be able to escape Ryan would be to leave on my own and then return later to save the children. (This lay at the core of my detachment.) He was always home, always with the children or never too far away. If I grabbed them and left in the middle of the night, I felt, I knew, he'd find us, hunt us down and prepare his reprisal. It was etched in my brain.

Ryan always told me, "I will die in a blaze of glory. In a police standoff—I see it. The police will come because I'm going to kill you. Because I'm going to kill the kids. And then they are going to kill me."

He was ready to murder all of us—and then go, himself, through suicide by cop.

So, you may be thinking, why didn't he just do it? Why didn't he manifest his dream and leave us all dead in our own blood? I'm not sure. I've asked myself that question a million times, and I don't have a definitive answer.

I think he liked the fantasy of it all, liked the power he had over us, over me, when he said it. He wanted his cake, and if he ate it, he knew it would all be over. I think, all these years later, he simply enjoyed having me fear him. I think he enjoyed abusing me, knowing he could get away with it and holding the power to keep us around. In that sense, I suppose, he had his cake and was able to eat it too.

Enough

"You cannot force the victim to leave. You must illustrate that you have an open door and safe retreat when they're ready."

My second son is named Conrad. Of course, Ryan chose the name. Conrad is Ryan's father's name, and he esteemed that man to a very high level. His father was law enforcement, and he'd had a distinguished career. Ryan was proud of this. In fact, his whole family was military—his ancestors having fought in nearly every war the United States has ever waged. Ryan boasted on this, this track record, this machismo, this power, the knowledge that his forebearers had killed, that they had killed and that it was an honorable thing to do. His family was American, as American as it got, he felt, and they'd achieved this title through violence and warfare.

Ryan was so enthralled by his 'American-ness' that he didn't even trace his lineage back to the old country. He was not Scottish American or Polish American or whatever-American. No hyphens. Simply American, so much so that on forms asking for ethnicity, Ryan would simply write in 'American.'

In Ryan's mind, his family was the cream of the crop, the American dream personified, the American ethos realized. His father would tell the story of having given Ronald Regan, then the Governor of California, a speeding ticket, "because that was the law."

Ryan was very proud of his father and rightly so. By every indication, he was a genuine and authentic good citizen and father. Regretfully, I never got the chance to meet him, same for my children. He died before I met Ryan, but I loved and respected the legacy of his father.

Thing is, Ryan's dad had this sixth sense about him. Just like Ryan. Another story, another true story, is that Conrad Sr. once found a bag of heroin—hidden deep in some secret compartment in a suitcase that no one else was able to find—with only his special knife and intuition. "I knew it was there, I saw the bag in there with my mind…"

And, as I said, Ryan had some powers, too. There was some magic to the family. That's what drew me to him in the first place. But magic can be dark magic. It can in fact, in Ryan's case, be evil magic.

Ryan opted for the military route after high school, wanting to join his family and make a name for himself in combat. But he never saw live action. While I can't say for certain, I feel that maybe haunted him a little bit, maybe led him to a feeling of needing to prove himself violently later in life. He was proud of his violent nature; he would tell me stories, for example, that in his high school yearbook he was voted 'last person you ever want to meet in a dark alley.' He took joy in people being fearful of him. On some level, it made him feel very powerful. In charge. In control.

He definitely exerted control over me. For a long time. Through all that I've recounted above and more so.

*

One day when our children were still very young, Ryan stormed into my office and started going after my receptionist. Down in the parking structure. He never liked her, never trusted her when he'd call and she'd say I was out of the office. Plus, she was in a relationship with another woman; this was not okay in Ryan's world. He came in (most likely to see me, but that was never clear) and they got into it. See, Ryan found out she'd been spending time with her ex, and he told her current partner about it.

My receptionist never liked Ryan before, and she definitely didn't like him after that.

Ryan saw her and started getting into it with her, over some 'filing issue' or something. He started yelling at her, face-to-face, and his yelling caused him to fling spit from his mouth onto hers. She spit back at him and Ryan headbutted her. Hard, with force—from an elevated spot near a drop-off in the parking structure, she was pushed backward to cascade over the ledge and strike her head on the concrete ground below.

She somehow retained consciousness and called the police. They were there in a flash and they put Ryan into handcuffs. He was barefoot. (He'd been so angry that he left the house barefoot, just got in the car and sped off to my office.)

Then Ryan bolted. He ran away, got a few feet of separation from the cop and went for it. Barefoot and in handcuffs, having just headbutted my receptionist over a wall in the parking structure, Ryan resisted arrest and ran. I don't like to think of who may have seen him running, what little boy or girl or mother or father may have seen him running the streets looking like a madman, or what fears it may have given them.

The cops finally caught up to Ryan and subdued him and took him in. He got booked. But he got off about a year later because he was going to push it to trial, and they didn't feel like they had enough for an open-and-shut case.

My receptionist did get a restraining order on Ryan.

That gave me something to think about, the obviousness of it—he hurt her, once, and she filed the order. That man had hurt me over and over and over and I had not.

The entire time we lived together, I was a practicing family and divorce attorney; I was in the easiest position to file and get a restraining order. But I never did. I thought about it a lot, but always came back to the understanding that Ryan was the type of person who just wouldn't follow it. That, and maybe I was too embarrassed to bring my personal life to work with me. I'm sure that played into it too, my ego, my desire not to show my colleagues what the man I chose was really like.

Until the next episode of darkness made me see the light.

Despite everything I've recounted, this next incident I'll recount was the most crazed I'd ever seen Ryan. He used to do these model airplanes, like, the 'buy the kit and build them yourself' type stuff. He'd build them, painstakingly, and then hang them from the rafters. He was very proud of them. One day, I came home and one of them was on the floor. "Did you throw this on the floor!" he snarled right as I walked in the door.

"No, Ryan, I did not."

"Well, if it wasn't you, it must have been Joshua."

Joshua was three years old. The models hung way out of his reach. "Ryan, Joshua can't reach that high."

He gave me that look, that red-crazed glare. I rethought my answer. I replayed his words in my mind: If I didn't lie and admit to it, he's going to blame Joshua. I made a snap-decision to protect my son and lied, told him that, yes, I must have thrown his airplane on the floor.

He came at me and grabbed me by my hair, the devil inside emerging. "Why did you throw my airplane onto the ground!"

He dragged me by my locks from the living room into the bedroom. It was late at night, the children already in bed. He grabbed a knife. Nothing new; I was used to that. I wasn't used to this: he proceeded to enter Joshua's room and cut a swath of our child's hair off and shoved the tresses into his mouth. Ryan then started chewing, chewing Joshua's hair. And then, in the most throated, guttural, demonic voice you can imagine, he draws out the word: "Inn-o-cent..."

He just stood there, crazy-eyed and chewing his son's hair and speaking in tongues. I looked at the man before me. I replayed the time we'd spent together, from that first night at the hotel through all the horror and right up to this moment. And I saw it. It clicked. The absolute insanity. Of it all. Of Ryan, of our relationship, of me having stuck around. It was the clouds parting to let the sun shine down. It was sight. It was understanding. It was a lot of things. It was the realization of the obviousness of the crazy.

I would get the restraining order. I knew I would.

I should have done it right then and there.

But for my sin of waiting, I suppose, I had to pay one more toll.

Later that night: more knives. Multiple stabbings. And then the wire coat hanger came out. This was the worst yet. Lacerations. Gashes. Deep cuts and gouges all over my back, blood spilling from my body. And then I looked out the corner of my eye and saw Joshua. He was looking at me. He was scared. And so was I, not for myself, but for him.

To this day, Joshua still remembers what he saw.

I'd had enough. My children had witnessed the horror and I was putting the wheels in motion to get the restraining order. I did, finally.

But then, it's hard to even say this now, but I kept dragging my feet, having second thoughts, convincing myself that Ryan would never follow the rules anyway and why bother? Why risk everyone finding out about my dark secret only to have Ryan walk through that paper wall and beat me even worse next time?

I shouldn't have dragged my feet.

A short time after, Ryan barged into my office and came at me and put his hands around my breasts and squeezed with the clenching power of a vice. So hard and such sharp pain. I screamed loud and wildly.

A paralegal from the next office heard the altercation. "What's going on in there? I'm calling the police!"

She did.

At my office.

It had been witnessed.

The authorities were called.

It was now or never.

I had to get out.

I filed the restraining order that afternoon.

"Ryan," I said, looking into his eyes, those eyes that could go from soft to demon in a flash, those eyes that drew me in with their charm and spit me out over and over with their hate, those eyes belonging to a man I now knew I had never really known, those eyes I was simply tired of looking at, the eyes of a madman. "Ryan—it's over."

Part II
Escaped

"I felt like I was hanging on by a thread. I thought that if I cut that thread, I would fall. It never occurred to me that If I cut that thread, I would fly."

The first few days after escape I kept asking myself, "Is this it? Is this the one?"

I mean, I had left before, only to return. Most people who leave abusive relationships don't do it on the first try. I was no different. "Is this going to be the one that finally sticks?"

I wanted it to be. More than anything else.

There was something new about this time, something different—I had told my family about it. I had put it out there, and my family knew what was going on. That was the biggest part of this escape plan; it wasn't just me going to a casino on my own or me checking into a hotel on my own. What made this escape different, what made it a true escape plan, was that I told my family what was going on.

And they took me in. And they wouldn't let me go back. Not this time. Not ever again. They talked to me and helped me to take a step outside of myself and see what was truly going on. They helped me see the obviousness of the situation. They helped me to be firm in my escape plan. They helped me see the light.

I also called Ryan's uncle, the one who wrote that letter to me in the beginning of my relationship with Ryan warning to be wary about getting involved with his nephew. I wanted

Ryan's uncle to know that I had left. He was happy for me. But he also called child protective services without me knowing.

I did not want him to do that. For a time, I was livid, distraught. Looking back now, of course, he did the right thing, so clearly so, but back then I didn't see it that way. I was drained. I was feeling like I was hanging on by a thread, and now I have to deal with a government agency and the investigatory steps I knew they would take?

I knew the law, which meant I knew there was a chance, however small, that his phone call could end up with me losing my kids. See, there is a point in domestic violence cases where, if the children have been witness to it, it becomes domestic abuse on them; it makes both parents liable, both parents neglectful, both parents seen as not protecting the children.

I was scared. But I knew I was on the right path of escape, and I knew I was in the right. I trusted the law to work like it should, so I cooperated with CPS on every level. They often get the short end of the stick, but their purpose is clear—to make sure the children are safe. I knew my children would be safe with me and I trusted them to do their jobs and make a sound judgement. I told them everything I could and worked with them to make sure all the appointments and therapy sessions were set up. I did everything with transparency; in the end they performed their service, and I kept my children.

And I was free of that man. I had escaped. My family had taken me in and I felt safer than I had in years.

I had known for a long time that I would have to do it, to leave Ryan, though for a long time I just didn't know how I would do it. It took having a plan and then, when the moment came, to follow throw on it and do it. I did. It took a lot of courage. It took a lot of getting over the shame, the fear, the embarrassment. But I had to—for myself and for my children—and so I did.

It was the beginning of a new world for me—a real 'first day of the rest of my life' moment. An awakening.

*

Still, it took a while to finally feel completely safe. To exhale and stop living with my breath held. To breathe. To stop the survival mindset and commence the thriving mindset.

To be fully transparent, I don't know if I will ever be completely without fear.

When I bought my home, for example, I made sure to buy one with a big, tall fence. In the neighborhood I ended up buying one in, that meant being on a side street to get around the community rules against tall fences. (Don't want the neighborhood looking like a ghetto, I suppose.) Though I loved some other homes, their fences were simply not high enough for me. That was why I didn't put offers on them. It wasn't the interior but the exterior. The walls weren't tall enough to keep my past out.

So, I bought the house on the side street with a big, tall fence. And the first thing I did was install security cameras. I won't tell you how many, but it is more than five. And once we moved in, the perimeter lights were kept on 24 hours a day. Even when I was asleep and the neighbors started to complain, those lights stayed on for a long time.

I had to heal. I had to learn that I was truly safe. I had to readjust my mindset and start looking forward instead of backward.

Now, those lights don't stay on 24 hours. I still have the big fence, but I can see the world beyond its walls.

Now I can turn my fear off. It may continue to run like some program in the background of your computer, there if I need it, there like our ancestors keeping alert for a grizzly bear or a mountain lion, but most of the time I can consciously turn it off.

Most of the time. But not always though.

Because of things like this: I have never given the father of my children the address to this home. But there they were, a few Christmases ago, his presents to the kids having been thrown over the fence.

He could have sent them to my parent's home like he'd done in the past. But he didn't. Why did he do that? To show me that he knew where I lived?

You answer for yourself.

Though some of the fear will probably linger for the rest of my days, the majority of my days, now—free of that man, escaped of that man—are lived in joy. And I am very thankful for that.

It feels so good to have moved on.

Masculine and Feminine

"From moment to moment, I can call

upon both my feminine characteristics

and my masculine ones on my own

terms, depending upon what the

moment calls for. It is not something

that takes over me anymore,

rather something I choose."

To protect ourselves, we develop different personas. I believe our mind does this for us, as another sort of barrier. For me, that manifested as toughness, masqueraded as toughness. I became cold. I became bitchy. I put on a real 'angry woman vibe,' all the time, and it was for real. Resting bitch face, scowls, quick to anger.

After a time, I realized I was coming off as hyper masculine—that I had, in many respects, become hyper masculine. I felt the absolute need to be strong, and so I masculinized because that's what had been imprinted on my soul as 'strength' at that time in my life. To be strong, I felt like I had to exhibit male characteristics.

It went pretty far. There were times, for instance, when I'd be talking with my male attorney colleagues and friends, after a case or something, and we'd be stroking our egos on how good we were and I would be like, "Yeah, let's not suck each other's dicks too much…"

Like the frogs in Jurassic Park turning female so life could "find a way," I was moving toward the masculine. So much so that it almost felt like I had a penis. I would obviously talk like I had one. And for a woman, this was a pretty big barrier to put up. I'm sure I could psychoanalyze it more for you here, I know I have, but suffice to say I recognized what I was doing. So much so that I began to dress hyper feminine. I knew what my interior was doing to provide me the avenue of the strength I thought I needed, so on the outside I became overtly feminine. I was always in dresses. I was always made up—painted toes, painted fingernails, eyelash extensions, everything. I came to a place where I did not own a single pair of jeans. Nope. Even though I was Cowboy Joe on the inside, no denim pants would be worn upon my legs.

Masculine on the inside, feminine on the outside.

For a long time, my mind chose those personas for me. Now, through a lot of self-work, I can vary my masculinity and femininity from a conscious place. From moment to moment, I can call upon both my feminine characteristics and my masculine ones on my own terms, depending upon what the moment calls for. It is not something that takes over me anymore, rather something I choose.

I think there is value in this. And I probably never would have gained so much range if I had not been put through the ringer so hard. It is another reason why I am who I am, today, because of what I have been through in my yesterdays.

Just like every single one of us.

All of our pasts have bad things in them. If we have lived more than a few years in our skin, we have been through some dark clouds. But dark clouds often come with those things we call silver linings.

The Absolute Illogic

"I made my escape.

It was the hardest thing

I'd done in my life.

It should have been easy.

It wasn't."

The custody case ended with me getting the children and Ryan facing the most restrictive visitation possibility: He could only see the children in a supervised visitation facility, with separate doors for both he and I, with a specific time to enter and pick up, and under direct supervision.

Yet as the years went by, Ryan's visitation rights sequentially increased. Not for the reasons you may think. Regretfully, the supervised visitation facility closed. There was nowhere local to go with the same services, so I chose to adapt. Because I had to. We would try out unsupervised visitation.

Also, by this time, the children were older. They had their own phones. They knew I would be staring at my phone until they got home safely. They could call me at any time.

To get my consent on the visitations, I worked with my children in empowering them to establish certain boundaries and safety protocols. We practiced them. And, above all else, I instructed Joshua and Conrad, over and over, that if anything ever happened, to tell me about it.

One day I was picking the boys up from a couple-hour hangout with Ryan at the mall. We figured that was one of the safe places for them to spend their time, lots of people around and such. I drove up and saw the three of them and parked my car to pick up my boys. Suddenly, Ryan hops in the car, too. "Give me a ride home," he states, there wasn't even a hint of an ask in his tone. Talk about boundaries.

When the kids were fourteen and twelve respectively, I finally said okay to overnights with their father.

I know, I was scared, too.

After the second one, I came to pick the boys up. And I'd made a mistake; I showed up with a hickey on my neck. We'd been separated for thirteen years, but it still irked him.

"You may want to cover up your neck," he said, "looks like the flesh-eating mosquitos were out last night."

We shared an awkward laugh. In the moment, he seemed to let it pass. Seemed to be okay.

But he wasn't. Later, those words came out again. That word 'Bitch.' That word 'Whore.' That word 'Cunt.' He closed with, "You just let your kids hang out with me so you can go whore around."

The overnights only happened twice. After the way he treated me after that second one, they were not okay. Because the next day it got worse.

He called me, angry. He'd had a fight with his girlfriend, and as a result they hadn't gone on a trip they'd planned. "You own me 3,000 dollars for this trip I can't go on."

The absolute illogic. "Ryan," I said, "I'm not talking with you anymore. You and your fight with your girlfriend are not part of my life. I'm blocking your number."

And I hung up.

So he started calling Joshua, telling him about his mom, telling Joshua what a bitch and a whore and a cunt she was.

Joshua came to me and said, so innocently and sincerely, "Mom, I don't want to be in the middle of this."

"That fight is between your father and myself. It has nothing to do with you," I told him. "You get to control your own boundaries—it's your decision. . . you can keep talking with your father, but you do not have to."

Joshua blocked his number. It's been a few years, and he hasn't changed his mind on that. Joshua does not talk to his father to this day.

Neither do I. And no more overnights.

Moving Forward

"No matter who we are or what we've

been through, I do feel that a

relationship with a higher power—

no matter the denomination or if you

call it 'the Universe' or even

'The Force'—helps us connect to the

Infinite and move forward here in our

walks on this earth."

Comparing my own children's childhood to my childhood, yeah, there were some obvious differences. And it wasn't just the money. It wasn't just the two loving parents that got along like best friends. My childhood was always organized. At its best, my children's was organized chaos. I ask myself why, and I come back to that one-word answer: Survival. That's the word that comes to mind. My relationship with their father was a mess, and it trickled into the household. It permeated the home.

I was trying to be everything to everyone. I spread myself too thin. Too much work. Too much trying to make a square peg in a round hole with my partner. Too much making up excuses for him.

People would ask, "what's wrong with him?" and I would make up excuses on the spot.

Even when he was there to answer the question for himself, I'd jump in and talk for him, make the excuses for him. It was a defense mechanism for sure. Everything was so messed up, and people knew it; the only way I could try to make it even palatable was to say that something was wrong, that he was having a bad day, that it was this or this or that. Something temporary.

Except, those were lies. Everyone knew they were. Even me. I just wasn't ready to see them for what they were. Until I finally did.

*

Conrad, despite being younger—I think it's impacted him more, the memories imprinted on him in a subconscious way. He can go from 0 to 60, from peace to ire in a second, then back to peace again. He's been to therapy, probably always will be on some level. His early years have been imprinted on him, the memories of life before we even know we are creating memories.

Joshua has always felt older than his age, perhaps made to grow up before his time.

I have healed, am still healing, and so are my boys. We are still moving forward, together, in many ways.

Church is a big component of our lives. I was raised in it and so have been Joshua and Conrad. Prayer groups are a part of our routine, part of our weekly forgiveness and self-love, part of who we are. Road trips and adventures are too. But we also enjoy our more grounding activities. Balance, I feel, is key to moving forward positively.

Joshua, my oldest, has a lot more ugly memories than Conrad. And Joshua, for good reason, has essentially asked, "If there is a God, mom, then why would he allow such bad things to happen in the world?"

I see his point. And I respect his journey. Joshua has, at times, declared his views as both atheistic and devoutly Christian depending on the season. He vacillates in his spiritual practice, and I am not going to force him to pick one view and stay with it. It is good to think critically, to wander and evolve, and so I encourage him on his journey.

Conrad has too. He's had similar thoughts to Joshua and yet he has found his way back into Christianity and is bathing himself in it. Almost to the extreme. I feel that he will continue to walk the path in his journey to understanding God and finding His way.

No matter who we are or what we've been through, I do feel that a relationship with a higher power—no matter the denomination or if you call it 'the Universe' or even 'The Force'—helps us connect to the infinite and move forward here in our walks on this earth.

I really do. I truly do. And at the end of the day, I know that the only judgment is God's judgment. It doesn't matter how other people judge me, how my colleagues or my friends or my family or you readers of this book judge me. Yeah, I want to be judged well by my peers here on Earth. But my relationship with God, His forgiveness, His blessings, are what ultimately matter most. And in my relationship with Him, I acknowledge that shame was holding me back, shame and fear. During my time with Ryan, I was hanging on by a thread.

And, I felt, that if I cut that thread I would fall—until I really got back in tune with the church, with its messages of forgiveness. It never occurred to me if I cut that thread to my past life and past experiences that I could fly. That I would fly. I didn't see it until I made the decision to snip that thread. I began to soar, and I liked it. It felt good to live free, to move forward untethered.

You can too, no matter the circumstances in your life right now—you can create your future. You can.

Love and Goodnight Hugs

"Two things helped me warm my heart

and allow that instinctual maternal

love to flow: prayer & meditation

and a deep commitment to continuous

work in self-improvement & self-help."

You may be lambasting me for how long it took to leave Ryan. And how long it took me to be firm on not letting him, in any level, back into my life. I know I have lambasted myself. That's part of the forgiveness thing. And I'm getting better at it, getting better at forgiving myself and making good decisions moving forward. For a while now, I've put boundaries in place not to let man in any shape or form into my life.

I've also erected boundaries to not allow another Ryan, a different man with the same plan, back into my life. But, a lot of these boundaries I put up, that my mind put up, caused other boundaries to be put up in other ways in my life. Like I said earlier, when I was with Ryan I always felt, knew, that one day or another I was going to have to run—and that I would have to run alone. And that caused me to put boundaries up with my own children. It took me a long time to see this and even longer to admit it. It's still hard to talk about it now.

For a long time when I would see other women with their children—the loving gazes, the hand holding, the natural embraces—it would pain me somewhere deep inside. I loved my children, but it wasn't that instinctual maternal love others seemed to display so effortlessly. I was almost robotic in my love: "Here's your food, here's this and that now go do that…"

I looked at myself as this cold-hearted bitch.

Two things helped me warm my heart and allow that instinctual maternal love to flow: prayer & meditation and a deep commitment to continuous work in self-improvement & self-help.

My kids had everything they needed: they were fed, they went to private schools, they always had the latest gaming console. But for a long time, they did not have the tender motherly love from their mom. I had to admit that. And once I did, once I recognized it and said it out loud, it helped me start to fix the problem. (Leaving a violently abusive relationship and beginning my healing journey didn't hurt either.)

Today, I am more loving. I am. I'll tell you that and my kids will tell you that. And it feels great.

Back before I healed, I'd sometimes even refer to my children to other people by numerical reference of birth, as 'Thing One' and 'Thing Two.' I know, sounds awful. It is clear as day to me, now, how messed up that manner of communication was. And sometimes I'd simply raise a finger when talking about them to someone—a raised index finger meant Joshua, an index and a middle finger meant Conrad.

In the 730 Child Custody Evaluation after Ryan and I's split, a doctor told me that Joshua had "an insatiable need for love." That my eldest son literally "could not get enough feelings of love and affection." Touch. That there must have been such a depletion of it in his life, his soul was telling him to fill up on it.

During that evaluation, the doctor also gave me an IQ test. I only missed one question.

"Beatríz," he said, "in twenty years of giving this test, only one other time have I seen such a score."

My IQ was there. Sufficed to say my Emotional Quotient, perhaps my Motherly Quotient, must not have been very high.

Today, I can see all the signs I missed back then. After Ryan was gone, Conrad literally always wanted to sleep in my bed with me. Like up until he was twelve years old when we talked about how he may be getting a little old for it. "You're almost a teenager now," I'd tell him, and he'd go try to sleep in his own bed. A half-hour later, he'd tip-toe back and curl up, fetus-like, next to me. I couldn't turn him away. And we'd sleep together, mother and child.

And Joshua? To this day, he still gives me about five or six 'goodnight hugs' per night. "Goodnight mom," he'll say, arms wide, and come in for embrace number one. Three minutes later: "Goodnight mom" and another hug. It goes on for a while. It's a pretty adorable evening routine.

And I appreciate those hugs too. Because it took us a long time as a family to get to this point. To move beyond our past and simply be able to hug. To touch without having to try. To instinctually show affection. To bond as we were meant to bond.

King Days and Fat Suits and Self-Work

"Part of my healing was learning that the journey is the destination."

A big part of my opening up to affection was through looking inward. I worked with a coach, a life-coach. Under his tutelage, I came to see how I was comparing myself to other women, to other mothers. Every time I looked at other women, my internal monologue would say, on repeat, "I'm falling short, I'm falling short."

I was so attached to how I looked, and I felt like I wasn't stacking up. I had to look like the personification of joy. That became a wall for me—to look like I was joyous on the outside, at all times, though I never really felt it on the inside.

Through my work with that coach and a steadfast practice of prayer and meditation, I finally realized that all I had to do with my children was just 'be.' To simply spend time with them. To not try to look like we were having a joyous time, to just be, and that the joy would come.

One thing we started doing was what we called 'King Days.' King Joshua Day or King Conrad Day, and whoever's day it was would get to pick whatever we do for that day—the only real rule that it had to be something we all got to participate in. It worked from the first time we did it two years ago, and it still does.

We go to the beach; we go on road trips. It's often pretty spontaneous: "Let's start by going to Subway," Conrad will say on King Conrad Day, and we'll get our subs and bring them into the car and then he'll just point a direction and we're off. No itinerary, just the journey. To the mountains or to the beach or a movie or a theme park. Sometimes all he'll say is "north!" and there we go. On the journey, together.

Before, everything in my life had to have a destination. "Today," I'd declare, "we're going to Disneyland," or "were going to the mall for two hours and then it is this, this, that, this, and that."

Part of my healing was learning that the journey is the destination.

And before I healed, sucks to say, I tried to show my 'affection' for my children through material items. Too often I was giving them things instead of hugs. They had the newest PlayStation before anyone else. They had new laptops and new 'kicks' (shoes) and new phones (yes, plural) all the time. Yeah, a new toy gifts satisfaction for a moment, but in the end, they leave a huge void.

Looking back on that behavior, I don't know how I got so dang materialistic. My parents weren't like that. I guess I was making good money and wanted to spend it, but still, I got caught up in the purchasing power of the American Dream—God Money, God Capitalism, God 'Things'—and it was not good. Not for me or for my children. For too much of their early lives.

And I have to say this, have to admit this one too: On some level, I loved work more than I loved my children. At least I showed work more love than I showed my kids. I was a lawyer, an attorney—that was cool, top notch, high-brow. I wasn't a waiter or a plumber. I wasn't a barista or a bellhop. A lot of ego became involved in my job.

At work, I had this feedback system to tell me I was good at it. People paid me a lot of money. I either won the case or I didn't. Most of the time, I did, which gave me reinforcement to keep doing what I was doing.

It became an easy way to avoid anything else. And my children—again, this is tough to say—but they often felt like 'needy little kids.' They didn't show me the same appreciation that my clients did. They didn't give me the respect that my colleagues did.

I got over that. Finally. Through readjusting myself and the way I lived, from the inside out.

I realized that I just wanted to 'be.' Just wanted to spend time with my children. With Joshua and Conrad. To hug. To watch a movie. To laugh. To live. To allow the love to flow.

*

And what about my 'love life?' Yeah, I turned that switch off. For a long time, I flat out did not trust myself to select another man, did not trust myself to bring another man into my life. I'd chosen poorly with Dan and made an irreparable selection with Ryan. "My radar must be off," I told myself. So I turned it off. To help keep it off, I put on a fat suit. A literal barrier between my heart and any potential suitors.

I gained 200 pounds. At least—I'm really not sure, the scale only went to 300lbs. At my heaviest, I think I was somewhere around 350. I genuinely didn't care. If I could still be good at my job, I told myself, that was all that really mattered. If I was a successful lawyer, no one could say a thing about my weight.

Until a doctor did.

I became severely diabetic. I had high cholesterol and bad blood pressure. I was having heart palpitations. At my weight and how much I was eating and how little I was exercising; I was ruining the mechanisms within my body. I was killing myself slowly.

"Lady," the doctor told me one day, "I don't know what else to say, so I will just say this: you are going to die—heart attack, stroke, whatever. You are killing yourself."

It was an eye-opening shock to hear those words.

So I started to care a bit more. I lost some weight. But I would yo-yo—I'd lose some then put it right back on. It was so difficult. It wasn't until, through more prayer and meditation and self-help coaching, that I full-on changed my mindset and took control of the situation to rid myself of the physical and metaphoric weight I was carrying around.

One of the biggest actions I took early on was doing a 30-day Green Drink diet: Only smoothies made from vegetables and a little bit of fruit. That's all I ingested. That and a lot of water. I lost 45 pounds in 30 days. It wasn't easy, but it was working. The 'diets' I'd tried before, limiting what I'd eat to only lose a pound or two per week wasn't tangible to me. When I saw the results of that month of Green Drink, it was tangible. And it started me on the path to getting my body—and my health—back.

Before that doctor said those words to me—"you are going to die"—food was what I had. I wasn't drinking or doing drugs. I wasn't allowing myself sex. What I could do to give myself a little dopamine rush was food. It felt like the safest thing. It was legal. Supermarkets and fast-food joints and all-you-can-eat buffets were everywhere. I could always get my fix. And so, I ate. A lot. And not much of it was high-quality calories. Food addiction became a real thing for me.

All that weight. You couldn't get close to my heart. You couldn't have even put your arms around me if you tried.

All I had been doing was working and eating. Eating and working. The diabetes got so bad—the come-down after eating so severe—that I even fell asleep at the wheel one lunch-hour after eating. And it was only a one-mile drive from the restaurant back to the office. Not good, Bea.

Losing the fat suit was part of the healing, part of releasing the weight, all types of weight, that I'd been putting on for so long.

Reconnecting

"I became addicted to work because it made me feel accomplished to help others. That saved my life."

When you're heavy, you don't take a lot of pictures. But a few do exist of me with the fat suit. If someone knows me from that time of my life and sees me now, they often don't recognize me. Some of the reactions are priceless.

"Oh, you must be Beatríz's daughter!"

And I'll tell them that, no, it's me. Just a lot less of me. A lot healthier and a lot happier me.

People tell me I look 20 years younger. I lost 200 pounds of fat and weight and history—and I've kept it off. For six years now.

My journey with food shed some light on why we eat. It became clear to me that humans only eat for three reasons: nutrition, entertainment, or addiction. I was eating for addiction. For the craving. For the high.

Now I eat from the space of nutrition. Well, about 95% of the time. I do allow myself a few 'entertainment meals' here and there. For me, it's all about intention, about knowing why and how I am eating. When I go out to a nice restaurant, I'll allow myself the meal, saying, "Okay, this is for entertainment. I am going to have fun tonight—and tomorrow it's back to salads."

"Mom," my kids will sometimes still say, "do you remember when you were fat?"

Their experience of me, for the first years of their life, was always of me laying down. I'd get home from work and straight off I'd head for the couch and recline. I was always tired. I was always running myself ragged and holding 200 extra pounds plain is not easy on the body. My knees hurt. My back ached. My breathing was heavy. Simply walking often seemed like a chore.

On my road back, movement and nature became big parts of my journey. I started hiking a lot. Once some of the weight was coming off, I even started trail running. Getting out into nature, being up in the mountains, is where a ton of that weight went. The natural environment—no concrete, no car horns, no emails—was so enlightening. So enlightening.

The beach, too. A lot of people don't know how many mountains surround L.A., but most folks know about the beaches. They're everywhere. Big ones, tons of sand to walk and run on. Just walking or jogging the beaches at sunset helped a lot. And just having fun. The beach brings out activity in us. Throwing a ball or a frisbee, playing volleyball or even just playing in the waves. And when we're moving for fun, when we're playing, that's easy exercise to get.

*

Before I found the fun and joy in movement and nutritional eating, I always had the feeling (the knowledge) that I was the biggest person in the room. Whenever we had to do a group photo, I always knew I would stand out as the fat one. The big one. The huge one. I didn't like it.

It was depressing.

They say that comparison is the thief of joy—and I was always comparing myself to everyone. I didn't compare well to the 'thin girls.' That was for sure. Even when I started the weight loss journey, all that work to lose a few pounds a week, it almost became harder. It was like I couldn't fulfill my addiction and I was still the biggest one in the room. It took a lot of persistence, persistence, and grit to truly walk the path. I started walking. One step at a time.

And here I am— Beatríz, 2.0. Lighter, more loving, joyous, from the inside out.

I even started going dancing again. Latin dancing, which means with a partner, a man, with his hands on your body as you move to the rhythms.

For a long time—though I'm Latina and I loved dancing—I just didn't. My best friend would invite me out, and when I had the fat suit on, I always made some excuse as to why I couldn't go. If she pulled my arm to the extent that I at least went over there with her, I'd sit in the corner with my

Kindle and a good heaping of 'resting bitch face' and try not to have fun.

I went eleven years without a man in my life. In any way. No male lovers for eleven years. I was just so scared, so afraid that "I couldn't trust myself."

Also, Joshua and Conrad even told me that they were okay with not having a male figure in their life. That, actually, they did not want another male figure in their life.

It has only been in the past three years that I've let myself date again. Let myself simply enter into a conversation with a man, let alone be touched by a man.

And allowing that touch back into my life was all part of my larger healing.

In my personal life and in my work life as a divorce and family attorney, all I had seen, all I had known, was family breakup. I saw it literally every single day. My work was seeing the breakdown of marriage, seeing the breakdown of relationships.

It became ingrained in me, so deeply, as firmly set as a marble statue. Until I finally started to chip away at it.

And to even begin considering letting another man into my life, I knew I had to open up to love. I had to start that journey of loving my children, of just 'being' with them. I know I've said it before, but my work with life-coaches helped so much in that. One of the major ways was through the teachings and simply being able, for the first time as a mother, to say out loud, "I don't love my kids as much as I should. I am cut off. I have all these boundaries..."

Saying it out loud allowed me to start sharing my story with others. It was the impetus I needed. I began talking to other people about what I had been through, about what I was still going through.

And they'd come up to me after I spoke. "Thank you for sharing your story," they'd tell me. "I'm going through the same thing you are."

It felt good. It felt good to share and it felt good to connect. To other women. To other human beings. To allow myself physical touch and emotional connection.

It felt good to know I wasn't alone. None of us are. More people love us than we know—more on that later...

Touch Therapy

"It's coming back to me,

how to put the nouns and verbs

in order, but complete fluency in the

language of love and vulnerability is still

something on the horizon."

So, yeah, I went eleven years without dating. Eleven years, no men. Not even a kiss.

I put on that fat suit, perfected my resting bitch face—put on every barrier and wall I could to make sure no one would even approach me. Light-switch, off. Consciously and subconsciously. If you were smiling at me too much, I was almost growling at you. If I got dragged to the bar by a girlfriend, I'd take my Kindle. Even to solo expeditions to the restaurant, I had it with me so I always had 'my out;' I could always say, "I'm reading" and at least look at the words upon the page so I would not have to interact with another man.

I needed to do this, to go a significant amount of time without a man in my life. I needed to find myself, to be the mom I needed to be. Just me and Joshua and Conrad.

Then, after a solid decade, I started to feel the need to heal myself. I needed to allow the possibility of opening up, even if just a little bit. I'd lost the fat suit and my resting bitch face had softened. I needed to feel touch. I needed sexual healing. I needed to feel adoration, some lovin', maybe even some love.

I know some girls who, after a breakup or a long spell away from the hairier sex, make it happen one-night-stand-style. One of my friends gave the eye to a barista and asked him, coyly, "want to help me move tonight?" I think the question pertained to moving furniture and stuff like that from her old place to a new one but the barista, ten years her younger and a few zeros lighter on the bank account, got the hint. And she got what she wanted. She got what she needed. Hopefully he did too.

One day I was ready. I went out dancing. By myself. No girlfriend dragging me along, no Kindle in hand. Latin dancing even, where the only way I know how to do it is to have the man's hands on my hips and move my body to the rhythm.

I was getting a drink at the bar, and I saw this guy out on the dance floor, dancing with another woman. My gaze just turned; I wasn't starting at him or anything, I just glanced at him as I scanned the floor. He smiled back at me.

I looked behind me, thinking he must be smiling at someone else. No one there. He smiled again. "Who's this guy smiling at?" I thought aloud.

Then, he smiled for a third time. No one else in my sightline. Yep, he was smiling at me.

I was confused—he was dancing with another woman. "Am I about to get hit up for a threesome?" I reached for my Kindle, but it wasn't there.

He smiled again and walked over. He approached, gliding across the dance floor toward me, that smile still on his face, and he introduced himself. We started talking. It was pretty loud and not easy to communicate. But we could tell that we both liked each other. He whipped out his business card and gave it to me.

A little odd, I thought, a bit forward. But I noticed that, while I may not have been fully embracing of the attention, I wasn't pushing it away either.

"Excuse me," he said quickly, "I have to go to the bathroom." And he smiled and walked away.

I twiddled my thumbs. He came back. With flowers. He gave them to me and said, "I'd really like to talk with you more, when it's not so loud. I'd love it if you called me sometime. When you're not with that guy."

Now I was really confused. I hadn't danced that much and hadn't really talked to anyone. I suppose there were men in my proximity, but—"What guy?"

"You're not with that guy?"

"I came alone, and I'll leave alone."

"Huh, guess I misread it."

Guess I did too, because I thought he was with the woman with whom he was dancing. (It was Latin dance, hands are everywhere.)

"Nice to meet you, Beatríz," he said. And he smiled again and we went our separate ways.

Not for long, though; I texted him that evening and said what a lovely gesture it was with the flowers, and how nice it was to meet him. Sending that text, I felt this wonderful mixture of being both a healed, self-confident woman and being sixteen-years-old and innocent.

Later that night, we went to dinner together. Me and another man! We ordered some drinks and started talking. At the dance club, we'd had to keep it short, almost curt because of the loud music, but at the restaurant we had both the time and the intimacy to open up into an extended conversation. We could talk softly. We could pause and absorb each other's words before taking our turn to speak. We could dance the dance of conversation. The drinks probably didn't hurt either.

Then, something in the window caught his attention. "Excuse me for a moment," he said. He stood from his chair and walked outside.

This guy is sort of odd, I thought.

Then he returned. Again, with flowers, just like at the Latin club. He'd found a street vendor and bought me flowers and given them to me. Then he gave me a kiss.

My first kiss in eleven years.

It must have been a good kiss. Actually, yeah, it was a damn good kiss. His lips stayed on mine and my lips stayed on his. Dormant tinglings within me erupted.

We started making out.

The bartender must have seen what was going on. Heck, the whole place must have seen what was going on. The bartender came over with the bill, "So, have a good night you two..."

She wasn't throwing us out of the restaurant, but she was kicking us out. She made it clear that it was time for us to leave. A little peck had turned into a wet kiss that didn't stop. Something inside of me had reawakened.

We started dating. Me and this man that had kissed me. We did the things that men and woman do. It felt good to be touched. It felt good to be back. It felt good to be healed.

It did.

But it's definitely still a work in progress to allow myself to feel completely vulnerable sexually. Simply to allow myself to be seen naked is not without its hesitations. Losing the fat suit—which I did through diligence and salads and a lot of self-love—left a lot of excess skin. So much skin, this 'other person of skin,' still on me, like some shadow that moved with me, trailed behind me as I swam. So I had some of the skin removed surgically. I did that for myself. I had worked so hard to get back into my normal body, and I wanted it to look normal.

I'm glad I opted to have the excess skin removed, but the surgery left more scars, scars of the proof of the existence of the biological blubber-wall I put up to protect me from being on the receiving end of any more knife-scars. Any more wire hanger scars. My naked body tells the story. Scars on top of scars. Some that will never fully heal. Many, as I've mentioned, in close proximity to my vagina.

And even more than moving beyond my acceptance and celebration of my body, I still have to work through a lot of trust issues. With other men. With myself.

With the choices I made in the past, it's difficult to take off the shield of vigilance—like, "How well do I ever really know someone?" I mean, in the beginning I thought Ryan was a good man. Dan too. Either they tricked me or I allowed myself to be duped. With men, now, I'm still sort of always waiting for the switch to flip. For the devil inside to come out to play. For 99% of men—for 99% of people—in the world, this isn't a warranted fear. But, for me, because of my past, I still fear I will gravitate toward that 1%.

Me and my body? I'm slowly working my way back into it. Into my feminine. Back into my goddess. Eleven years between kisses is a long time. A long time to not speak a language. It's coming back to me, how to put the nouns and verbs in order, but complete fluency in the language of love and vulnerability is still something on the horizon. Something I can grasp at times but don't yet hold.

    Someday.

High Times

"For me, Latin dancing comes down to trust. I trusted the partner.

I finally surrendered.

And in surrendering, I trusted myself."

The only way to do Latin dance is 'hands on body.' There's no other way. It's a passionate act. It's a dance among dances—one that involves actually touching another human being other than your kids. It means letting other human beings, oftentimes men, touch you. Not what I was into after leaving Ryan.

But my best friend is just one of those humans with *la música* in her blood. And she's persistent. "You have no idea how fun it is, Bea. You have to come with me. You have to!"

So, I went with her. Not very often, but I did. That's when I'd even bring my Kindle along so I'd have an escape route, an exit strategy from another human being trying to interact with me.

Whenever someone managed to get me on the dance floor, I'd stiffen. When that man (wouldn't have mattered if it was Brad Pitt) put his hands on me, I'd stiffen. Immediately.

By this point, I'd undoubtedly have had a couple drinks. Some liquid courage to at least start moving my feet. And I'd get this feeling—this feeling of extreme anti-trust, of fear; I'd literally start asking myself, "Is this man just spinning me around and around to get me more drunk?"

Fear. Fear of losing control. Fear of men. Fear of being a woman. Fear.

I needed to get over it. I needed to be able to dance. In Latin dance, the man leads, and at that point in my life ten years later, I was still unable to be led. Too much giving up control. I would literally say—in my head and sometimes even to the man in front of me—"you're doing it wrong!" even though I knew it was all on me, all on my lack of trust.

If I became better at the dances themselves, I thought, maybe that would help things out. If I got better at the steps and learned to feel the rhythm like my BFF did, maybe, just maybe, I'd feel confident enough to not project my fears onto the next man who put his hands to my hips to music.

So I started going to Salsa class. I wasn't a great dancer. (Being Latina, that's not easy to admit.) But at least I was giving it the old college try.

This one time I showed up to class early. The traffic had been light, I hit all the greens, and I'd arrived early. Then I remembered I had something else green in my car. I had forgotten to take some weed out of my trunk after my last girl's night out. I thought, why not?

I retrieved the little jar and pipe and took a couple tokes. I listened to some music in my car for a few minutes and then opened the door and floated into Salsa class.

I walked into the studio not feeling anxious. Not feeling the stress of 'having to try to be feminine and move my body.'

I was relaxed. Super relaxed, in my own little world that Venn diagrammed with others around me, and the music in the air. I wasn't 'fighting it' anymore. Little Beatríz got to come out and play. I was childlike, open and free and unthinking. I went by feel, feeling feminine, moving my feet and shaking my hips. I was sassy as heck and smooth as flowing water.

I let myself be led. A man's hands on my body, spinning me around and looking into my eyes. I trusted myself and so I trusted my partners.

I surrendered. And it felt so dang wonderful.

*

I have to say that my state of mind is what allowed me to do so. And I'd have to say that the marijuana—that ancient plant we humans have been smoking for so long—worked its magic to help me slow down my mind and speed up my feet.

My experience that evening empowered me to break down barriers. It allowed me to break down barriers I'd put up that needed to come down. And now I can Salsa, sober, no mind-altering agents needed, in any room I walk into, because I broke them down. Because I altered my mindset permanently.

I'd seen that I could do it, that it was fun, that dance was part of who I am. And that I should trust myself to do it. To move, to be led, to dance. To feel relaxed and free.

The King of King Days

My children.

My sons.

They started singing the mantra as well.

"Easy day! Piece of cake! I got this!"

One of the things my children and I share and celebrate is our love of 'the road trip.' We embark upon them constantly, spur-of-the-moment, on whims and fancies, wherever we want to go.

I want Joshua and Conrad to feel that they can do and go whatever and wherever they want. I want them to feel utter freedom. I want them to feel that nothing, no one and no thing, can hold them back.

And, opting for so long to remain a single parent, I think I have overcompensated on 'the male.' I feel that my boys need some traditional masculine experience—and I endeavor to give them that. My boys will not be deprived of anything.

So, one day a couple years ago, it was King Joshua Day, and we were off to the rugged wilds of the Arizona badlands to do some ATVing.

This was no go-cart track. This was the real thing.

The waivers to sign looked like something I'd give a client at the office. Thick. Every scenario you could think up and more. Oodles of fine print. I perused them and signed them and handed them to the guy who was giving us All Terrain Vehicles with lots of horsepower to go out into an untamed wilderness.

"And remember," he said, cool but stern, "if you get in trouble, the only rescue option is helicopter—and it's not cheap."

We were to do whatever we wanted, go as fast as we could, as long as we followed the certain colored flags marking the course so we would find our way back.

"Alright," I said, and off we went, two young teenagers and their masculine-prepped mother.

Joshua and Conrad revved their engines like it was the Indy 500. They shot out ahead, out of the gates and into the boulders and dust. Fast. Faster. I knew I had to keep up. I had to maintain their pace, couldn't have them leave my sight. I pushed down on the throttle beyond my comfort zone and off I went, zoom, zoom-bump-bump-zoom!

I was having fun but I was also a little scared out of my mind. I'd never done anything like this before—not this untamed, not this fast, not with this much power between my legs.

I thought we'd be following someone, a guide, something. Nope. Not even another ATVs in sight. Just us. Just us three out in the wildlands.

I thought the colored flags would lead us on a straight and easy path. They did not. It was rocky terrain that would bounce you around like a tectonic plate, bouncing you off course and making you execute split-second steering maneuvers to get back on course, so you didn't tip over and crash and burn.

Faster we went.

I started sweating. Puddles, the beads dripping down my back to pool on the seat. I became scared. Frightened. It was bordering on paralysis. Then a mantra came, just came to me or from within me, from Jesus or from the Buddha or from the ancient spirits of the Southwest. The mantra came to me, and I began to recite it: "Easy day. Piece of cake. I've got this."

Joshua and Conrad, those daredevils, even came to feel the power of the machine and the unforgiveness of the terrain. They, too, started to feel weight of the consequence of a wrong turn, a flipped ATV.

We came to realize that were all in a little over our heads. But 'in over your head' can be a great place for growth. 'In over your head' can teach you how to swim.

I floored the pedal and caught up to them, now singing my mantra loudly, defiant against the harsh boulders and rattling rattlesnakes. "Easy day! Piece of cake! I got this!"

Joshua and Conrad heard me. They picked up on it. My children. My sons. They started singing the words as well. "Easy day! Piece of cake! I got this!"

We were all singing in tune, our voices and the din of the motors in the barren wastes of Arizona. Despite our positive affirmations, there was a point where I genuinely thought I might die. Where I thought we all could.

It was a steep incline over a gnarly crag. Steeper than anything we'd yet had to tackle, with impassable boulders on either side and a drop-off into a sharp left hand turn on the other side. I knew I'd have to gun it to get up the near-vertical wall so the machine wouldn't flip the front-end and come crashing back down on me. But I couldn't give it too much throttle or else I'd fly off the acme and miss the do-or-die downhill left-turn!

In a millisecond judgment of instinct—instinct from where I did not know because I'd never done this before—I throttled the engine and bounded up the incline, pulled the steering wheel hard-left, bounced up and down in the pool of my own sweat and came out the other side right where I needed to be, all the while screaming, "Easy day! Piece of cake! I gotttt thhiiiissss!!!"

I had shown my children the way, shown them that it was possible and so they knew it was possible. They listened to their instincts and gunned their engines and bounded up the wall and came down it and into the hard-left like leopards on four-wheels.

And then we bounded down the road together, confident and fast and free under the beating Arizona sun, singing, "Easy day… Piece of cake… We got this!!!"

*

We followed the colored flags and finished the trek, making it back to the starting point. We shut down the engines and unmounted our steeds like characters from the Wild West. We had done it. We had conquered. We had returned. No helicopter needed.

"Mom," Joshua spoke to me after a time, "we could've died out there today, huh?"

I looked at him and absorbed my son's words. "We could have, Joshua—but we didn't."

"How'd we do it?"

"Courage," I said.

Then all three of us dove into a discussion of that word. Of the word, 'courage.' And of overcoming fear. Of the 'scared shitless moment,' and what it can teach us about ourselves and about life and about how to get through it and move forward.

The conversation drifted well beyond ATVs and crag rock into past memories and future hopes.

It was beautiful healing. Healing created by doing. Healing created by action. Healing created by us. On King Joshua Day.

Part III
Manifesting

"... and what does your life get to look like once this case gets to be over?"

I have an academic interest, and a background, in Women's Studies. That was my focus in my undergraduate education, what my B.A. is in. As a young girl, I was always fascinated by America's suffrage movement, by Susan B. Anthony and the Seneca Falls Conference. I liked Joan of Arc, read more than a little about Frida Kahlo, Maya Angelou and Harriet Tubman. I pursued the study of women's history in school, and I have always endeavored to 'be there' for women in life. But in my research into understanding my own abusive relationship, I came to see how it is not just women who get abused in relationships—and that abuse comes in a variety of forms. I'm going to give a TED Talk on this someday, someday soon. It's a goal of mine, and it's within reach. (Look me up and hold me to this.)

What I'll speak about will be drawn from my life, drawn from some of the pages of this book. And it'll be about the most abusive relationship not being the one we have with our abuser, but the one we have with ourselves—and about the toxic forgiveness we allow ourselves to give.

For me, it manifested as overworking and not being present for myself, which led me to not being the mother I should have been for my children. It manifested as my relationship to the toxic forgiveness that I kept extending to Ryan. It manifested as the shame I put on myself.

"And the only way to change," I'll say up on that stage, "is by asking the questions and changing the answers in our head. The only way we can change the relationship we have with ourselves is by amending the language patterns of how we talk to ourselves—and a lot of that comes with intention."

See, we must be intentional with how we talk. Intentional in how we talk to ourselves and in how we talk to others. I learned an acronym a while back that really helps me do this: W.A.I.T. It stands for Why Am I Talking. And it helps me think before I speak. If I don't W.A.I.T., I have the tendency to go on autopilot and simply say words. A lot of us do this. And that is not speaking. It is just making noise.

In my life-education and self-help work, I have worked with many wonderful doctors and special human beings. And I have learned a lot of intriguing things.

One of them is how I have learned to manifest things into my life. I have grown to be able to get intentional about my thoughts and to create what I envision. I have awakened to the fact that I can ask the universe for gifts. I can visualize where I want to be and what I want to be doing—and make it happen. Whether in my head or kinesthetically, I can, and I am, bringing great things into my life.

My manifestations are declarations to the universe of what I want to happen and declarations to my body that it can happen.

Down in Arizona, there's this scientist who works with people who've become paralyzed. Against everything we've been taught by the textbooks, she gets them to walk again. It is amazing. And she does it through self-speak. She moves people to walk again by having them tell themselves they will walk again. She gets people to walk again by having them change the language they speak to themselves.

"It's all about your mind hearing your words and your body hearing your words," she'll say. "When we say something—when we tell ourselves what we will do, how we will do it, and when we will do it—and then go do it, we grow in the capacity to keep manifesting."

Self-talk is neural-pathway stuff. It is biofeedback stuff. It is 'the ability to predict the future stuff.'

I knew, from early on after my escape from Ryan, that self-talk and manifestation worked for me. I could see the results in my own life and so I knew it did; but when I learned there was actual 'science' behind it, it floored me. It blew me away. And it helped my scientific mind believe what my body already knew.

See, my mind is a funny thing. I've always been a good learner, but I've always learned fairly differently than other people.

When I watch a movie, for instance, I often turn off the sound and put the subtitles on. Sort of odd, right? No audio, no voice inflection, no background music. But that's how I learn. On the learning spectrum, my graph is off the charts slanted toward the ultra-visual.

We are all so different. All of us. Some people learn better through audio pathways. Others in kinesthetic ways. Me? Almost exclusively visually.

And so, I am a reader. When I see the words on the page, my mind instantly and sometimes extravagantly begins to interpret them into images. That's the visual.

I will never be able to play a piece of music simply by listening to it like some people I know, but I can paint a picture with my mind. And, though I'm not Matt Damon in Good Will Hunting or anything, I do have a fairly photographic memory. This helps me in my work as an attorney as well as in my coursework with abuse victims. It helps me learn from moments in my own history so I will not be doomed to repeat them in the future.

I remember what I have been through. And my memory will never let me enter into that type of relationship ever again.

*

With all of my continued self-help education about how I learn and live, I bring a lot of what I've learned into work with me now.

I used to be all business. All documents and precedents and rulings. Now I bring a larger scope to the office with me. I bring a more well-rounded attorney, a more well-rounded human being to my clients.

"… and what does your life get to look like once this case gets to be over?" I'll ask now and help my client manifest good things into happening in their larger lives.

It used to be all about spousal support and the client screaming to me about "that ex of mine!" My approach is much more wholistic now. I bring a lot of emotional and spiritual reservoirs to my work now. With all I've been through, I've come to see a larger version of the world. A more layered version of the world. A world in which I am here to help—in any possible way that I can.

Like the time I was getting some beauty treatment and the gal and I just started talking. I told her a little of my story, some of the things I'd endured in this life. And from my opening up to her, she opened up to me. She told me how she had basically been kidnapped and raped, for days on end, by the father of her children. It had happened years prior, and she'd never really told anyone about it. She had been holding in the shame, the embarrassment of having someone close to her doing something awful to her.

"If it would have been a stranger," she confided, "it would have felt different." And then we talked, then we helped each other.

She felt comfortable enough to talk to me, to open up about her past trauma. And that may have been the start of the healing process for her. That's a lot of what I do with my life now.

A sus órdenes, just like I was back in preschool.

Gene Keys and Gibran and Gods and Goddesses

"Your joy

is your

sorrow unmasked."

- Khalil Gilbran

In his book, The Gene Keys, Richard Rudd outlines for us an invitation to commence a new journey within our life. His message is clear and profound, and it has helped thousands of people since its publication.

Rudd speaks from a perspective of "wisdom rather than knowledge." Knowledge, he states, is something you learn and that you've studied yourself, something you've inhaled—while wisdom is something unwound and unlearned, something you exhale rather than breathe in.

I agree with him on this. In living, whether in an abusive relationship or in simply attempting to maneuver the stresses and obstacles of everyday life, wisdom is the path upon which we must endeavor to travel. We can't always glean what to do from some data in a textbook, but we can absorb words and concepts from works like Rudd's to exhale out the wisdom we need.

In chapter ten, Rudd speaks upon the fourth gene key, the power to read and solve logical patterns—the ability to universally understand the rhythmic tendencies of life, of this world, and then to predict them. We can all do this; we all have the language of nature and the universe within us. It is just that many of us have lost the ability along the way.

This is because, at a low frequency—the frequency of reaction rather than absorption and exhalation—we often distort the logic of a situation, bending the facts with our minds. We see things how we want to see them rather than how they are. We see the things that corroborate our predetermined point of view rather than looking for the absolute Truth in a situation.

If we are having a bad day, for example, we will find ways to support continuing that bad day. If we don't like someone, we will compile a list of why, yeah, that person is unlikeable.

We will find support for what we believe rather than seeking the truth behind the facts.

We all do this; we do this with our political and religious beliefs, with how we chose to live our lives against how our neighbors chose to live their lives. The mid-20th century author and Nobel Prize winner, John Steinbeck, said it like this: "No one wants advice, only corroboration."

I'd have to agree with him.

And to get back to Rudd, this slanted perspective of truth, the slanted perspective of logic, can lead us down dangerous paths—because we are giving the mind, the ego, the authority to make important life decisions. And, as it has also been said, we don't experience the world, simply our own central nervous system. When our perceptions of the world become illogical, that must be checked.

When we live in a reactive state, an emotional state (like speaking before W.A.I.T) unresolved emotional patterns are taken up by our mind and built into an elaborate framework—our mind convincing our mind—and that overshadows the truth of the situation. When we live reactively, our opinions and resentments and judgements become solidified as certainties. As absolutes.

This is how we blind ourselves. It is how I blinded myself. I didn't have the perspective to get out of my head and look upon my situation from afar. My ego and my own central nervous system were looking for corroboration rather than truth.

With other people's relationships and actions, we can see them so clearly—what is right, what is wrong—but when it is us, we are too often simply 'too close' to see it.

Like the bee stuck in your kitchen and trying to get back outside; he keeps flying into the glass of the window, over and over and over, when all he needs to do is back up a bit, take stock of the situation, and fly ten inches to the right to where the window is open to the outside world.

We humans, especially those of us in abusive relationships, are all too often like this bee. We can become deluded, blind, distorting the picture or just not seeing it clearly.

My situation was clear as day. Ryan was beating me constantly. He came close to killing me. Needless to say, it was not healthy. I should have left. But, for too long, I did not.

I had come to form a distorted the logic of the situation. I had told myself the story that "it wasn't that bad." And I told myself that story so regularly that I came to believe it as the truth.

Pretty distorted stuff.

We all have the power within us to objectively assess a situation from all sides. We have the power within us to take off the blinders and see what is actually going on.

Just like with science—to be truly objective, it must be open to all arguments and counterarguments. You cannot go into the lab with a desired outcome in mind; you must go in with objectivity and distance.

You can't know what you know before you know it. That is being blind. And that is dangerous—whether it is some sort of fringe political or religious belief or the story you are telling yourself about your abuser being "not that bad."

The power that wisdom gives us is the perspective to see all sides—giving us the ability to take off the blinders, to identify the fear, and see the situation as it is. Wisdom and perspective allow us to see our own lives with the clarity that we see others'. Wisdom and perspective, though they can take time to grasp, allow us to look at our situation with untainted logic and make the step-by-step decisions to do what must be done.

We human beings are not bees. We do not need to keep hitting our head upon the glass window when there is open air just a little bit away.

*

Richard Rudd is a profound and positive influence on many people in today's world. He is still alive and speaking his message. Another writer and philosopher who lived a long time ago—but who still keeps influencing the world and elevating its wisdom—is Khalil Gibran. In his seminal work, The Prophet, he tells how "your joy is your sorrow unmasked."

What does he mean by that? What do those words mean to you?

To me, the statement speaks to the yin and the yang of things, to the ebb and the flow of things, to the capacity to feel in equal and opposite ways. Like a wave that draws water out into the sea in order to rise and white-cap and crash it back upon on the shore, our capacities are dualistic; the more sorrow we have, for instance, the more joy we can then feel.

And once the veil of sorrow is lifted, our joy can reign.

When we feel the temptation to say "woe is me" during a bad day or even a bad week or time of our lives, we must remember that even for how low we feel right now, we will feel commensurate, equal and opposite joy on the other side.

If it was never rainy, we wouldn't cherish the sunshine nearly as much. If we never experienced sorrow in our lives, the joy would not be as sweet.

If you have had to endure an abusive relationship (or especially if you are still enduring an abusive relationship) I encourage you to hold on to Gibran's words: "Your joy is your sorrow unmasked."

Yes, this time of sorrow is nothing but a mask. It is not you. It is not who you are or what your life is. It is a polaroid snapshot, not the whole movie. And you can tear up that polaroid and throw it away to live your happy ending.

With the sorrow you have gone through, the joy that you will be able to feel—to experience, to radiate and live and celebrate on the other side—will be immense.

And we are all still writing our story.

In mythology, we learn a lot about immortals. About gods and goddesses and their adventures and conquests from the heavenly realm and into the earthly realm. But these gods and goddesses lack one thing that we mortal humans do—mortality, the knowledge that our days of breathing fresh air and watching sunsets is limited. The knowledge that we will one day die.

While this may sound morose, it is not. Our life cycle is something to be celebrated. It is something we have that the immortals of our stories and our religions do not have. And, because of this, we have something over those celestial beings—the ability to live in the moment and enjoy each second for the precious gift that it is.

We know this life will come to an end one day. Even if we believe in reincarnation or the immortality of the soul, our flesh and blood has a down-ticking clock built into it that cannot be denied. Unlike immortals, on some level we know we are living on borrowed time—and that gifts us the power to seize the moment, to turn negatives into positives, to stop simply surviving and start living before it is too late.

Gibran goes on to complete his passage of "your joy is your sorrow unmasked" as this:

"When you are joyous, look deep into your heart and you shall find it is only that which has given you sorrow that is giving you joy. When you are sorrowful look again in your heart, and you shall see that in truth you are weeping for that which has been your delight...

"Some of you say, 'Joy is greater than sorrow,' and others say, 'Nay, sorrow is the greater.' But I say unto you, they are inseparable. Together they come, and when one sits alone with you at your board, remember that the other is asleep upon your bed."

There is a lot of Truth to this wise philosopher's words. They can be read and reread, and probably should be.

So, the next time you are having a bad day, think about Gibran and gods and goddesses. And know that when your sorrows are unmasked, they will offer wings of joy upon which to soar.

Unexpected Life Lesson

"If a grown woman wants to get beaten every day, that's her decision."

Once, when I was young—before I ever met Ryan or had become a practicing lawyer, when I was still climbing the ladder and still relatively innocent—we had this temp bailiff come in to work. Real nice guy. And he opened up about this abusive relationship his daughter had been in.

"What did you do about it?" I asked, thinking he was going to tell me how he went in and beat the guy to a pulp.

"Nothing," he said. "I didn't do anything. If a grown woman chooses to get beaten up every day, that's her decision."

"Woah," I mouthed, shocked.

"I told her that I am here for her. You know I told her that. And I told her, you know, 'when you are ready, you always have a place to come home to.'"

"She ever take you up on it?"

He looked at me and shook his head. "Not yet."

Little did I know how this lesson would prove so true in my own life on down the road. Let's dig into this in the next chapter.

Why Victims Don't Get Help

"They are made to do this out of fear.

But it doesn't have to be this way"

Post Covid, the reality I can speak of from my own experience working with family law is the obvious and steep rise of abuse and separation.

The pandemic was tough on individual people for a lot of reasons. It was tough on relationships for a lot of reasons. One of those reasons is that people were simply made to spend so much time together. Our routines became broken, the things we did outside the house canceled; for long periods of time, we had to stay at home, in constant contact with our chosen partners. Partners we had not chosen to spend this much time with.

In normal times, we find a way to stay busy, to be out of the house, to ink-in time throughout our days to be physically away from our husbands and wives. To not see each other. For a lot of people, it's going to the gym right after work so they don't get home until just before dinner. It's a boys' night out or a hike with the girls. It's bingo night or a ballgame.

When those things were taken away, when we were forced to stay home and all the little quirks and antics and annoyances were accumulating and driving people nuts, it created tension in a lot of relationships. High-level tension, and when that tension came to light, many relationships went one of two ways: either people decided to leave, to end it, or the violence reared its ugly head.

Domestic abuse rose significantly during 2019-20. What the actual numbers of domestic violence abuse were, we can only guess. But, the Los Angeles Police Department reported responding to 16% more calls in April 2020 than in April 2019 . And Orange County authorities reported 25% increase in domestic violence calls during Covid-19 stay-at-home orders . If this is any indicator to the rest of the country, to the rest of the world, needless to say, it is a big problem.

When people came to be 100% in the home, many partnerships could no longer hold on. Plus, a lot of people lost their income, were forced to stay home because of lock downs—and coupled with the stresses of having no money, things snapped. From that point on, what occurs? Domestic violence. Abuse.

That's what I saw in my office, and those are the stats across the board. The facts. When we had to see our significant others more, nearly all the time, shit hit the fan. When he's never gone, when she's always home, when I can't even take the kids to school or go to the gym, when I can't even make a phone call without thinking or knowing someone can hear me—what do I do?

"I'm always at home," I would hear. "I'm always with my partner."

Things got ugly.

In my practice, I started taking cash for my consultations. Because a lot of women were seeing me for services (mostly through telephone or internet meetings), and I learned a lot about how their partners were tracking their cards, reviewing their statements. When 'Law Office' popped up on the statement, metaphoric and literal punches were thrown.

I remember one consultation, right after I was finally able to meet face-to-face with clients again. I was working with this woman, and we were making some good progress. Things were going well. Then her phone buzzed. She looked at it. Her demeanor changed instantly. "He found me," was all she said, and her face went white.

She stood up and left the room, and I never heard from her again. Never saw her again. I think about her often, and I hope she is okay. I wish I could have convinced her not to go.

I often now even hesitate to call or text a client, knowing that partners check the phones of their significant others, keeping tabs on the incoming and outgoing calls and texts.

"I put a tracker on her phone," men have told me like it is no big deal. Almost like they're proud of it, having realized the obviousness of the idea. "So, yeah, I know what she's up to, who she's seeing."

Know this: Technology can be a supportive tool, helping us interact with friends and people online and through calls and text, but it can also be made to snag us. Because most everyone goes most everyplace with their phone in their pocket or their purse. If you are in an abusive relationship, just know that this sort of thing happens.

I encourage people to memorize important phone numbers in their life. Or at least to have a handwritten list of the numbers you'll need if you are forced to start going places without your phone on hand. Also, to get some good physical maps and put them securely in your car. And to carry cash—always carry cash because you never know when you're going to need to pay for that cab or that hotel room or even that plane ticket without someone finding out about it who you don't want finding out about it.

I know women who escape the house like this: they'll hail a taxi, go to the mall, walk around for fifteen minutes or so, then get into a different taxi to get out of there. People are made to live like actors in a suspense-film in their everyday life.

They are made to do this out of fear. But it doesn't have to be this way.

*

To get a restraining order—and I could go way more into the details here, but I won't—I'll just say that to get a restraining order one does not need a high level of proof. The writ is not held to as high of standards as some other actions because the law knows that proof doesn't exist in a lot of cases, that in the cases of abuse and domestic violence it has often been hidden or otherwise made to disappear. The restraining order exists largely to support women.

I could have got a restraining order in a flash. I didn't. Not for a long time. I thought of it as "a piece of paper that he would just walk through." That was one of the reasons why I didn't get help.

I go more in depth in my Toxic Forgiveness Course, which can be found at www.beatrizpelayogarcia.com/course/, and I will just touch upon some of the reasons here, some of the things I've identified, on why victims of domestic abuse don't seek help:

- We don't recognize what is going on as both illegal and abusive behavior.
- We can't believe the story.
- A lot of times, every single movement and communication is being tracked, which causes further paralysis.

- Money—a lot of victims, especially women, are kept in places of low economic-freedom. They don't have the money for the divorce, let alone a simple $100 consult with a lawyer.
- The feeling that "calling the police will escalate the situation."
- A restraining order is not bullet proof. It is not a shield. It is a piece of paper that can be walked right through—especially by someone who is not a law-abiding citizen (which, let's be honest, most abusers aren't).
- The abusee is fearful that once 'next steps have been put in place' the abuser will see it as a blank check to be written out in even more violent ways—seen as reprisal for 'going public' with the secret.
- The Bible, and other religious doctrine, don't condone leaving a marriage.

Let's go deeper on this last one and then into a few more:

I have literally heard family and friends tell people—abusees, men and women in the throes of terrible psychological and physical violence at the mouth and hands of their spouse—that, "All couples go through this. Human beings have tempers, God hates divorce... if there isn't cheating, then the Bible says you have to stay."

Oh, and if you've ever read it, the Bible does not condone abuse by males onto females. Even in other civic doctrine, the Rule of Thumb has often been interpreted to mean that men can beat their women, in fact he can and should if she won't listen, just as long as the stick or weapon is not larger than the measure of the width of your thumb.

While many of us hold the Bible and other books and doctrine as the word of God, we also must acknowledge that some of the text serves an antiquated social construct. The equality of woman, for example, has taken a long time. We didn't even get the right to vote in the United States until 1919; gender equality is still, unfortunately, a relatively new historical concept.

And part of the antiquated context of Christianity (as well as Islam and others) is the idealization of martyrdom. It elevates the act of self-sacrifice to the highest level. I mean, that's what Jesus did, right? So, all of us worshippers of him should strive to, as well?

Not in the face of an abusive relationship. Each and every life deserves to be lived, deserves to be lived freely and happily.

Speaking from the realm of the woman here, I will state that many of us surrender our power to our partners/husbands, and a lot of that power-surrender pertains to money—how it comes in and what and where it goes toward. In our world, with its capitalistic construction, money, on some level, equals freedom. Without it, you cannot hop on a plane to faraway lands or even put gas in your car (if you have a car) to get out.

The financial-freedom equality between men and woman needs to change. We all have uniqueness and power within us; we can all make some money. We don't need a lot, and endeavor to put some away for yourself in case you ever need it.

I would also add here that a real reason people stay quiet and remain in relationships is because of a belief in change. This belief (which I held onto) that people can and will change—the hope that at some point "he's going to wake up from this, that at some point, he'll get better, be better"—is a sick hope.

Previous action dictates future action. What has happened, what is happening, will continue to happen. That is the reality of the situation. While the dates on the calendar change, a human's nature—the things they do and why they do it—largely remains constant.

Abusees are also reticent to leave because of the fear of depriving a child of a mother or a father. Yes, most abuse is still at the hands of a man to a woman, but it goes the other way, too. It happens in same-sex marriages and in polyamorous marriages. It happens from human being to human being. Even from human being to their pets. But the fear of leaving a child without a father, to me, was one of the blinders that kept me from moving on, kept me from leaving, kept me from escaping.

"To me, he's the devil," I would think, "but to Joshua and Conrad, he's sometimes, even often, 'a good dad.'" I made myself believe that, talked myself into believing it.

I was wrong. While he could make them laugh and provide some male influence, the plain truth is that nobody is a good father when they abuse the child's mother. Period. Fact. Truth.

To piggyback on this, in my relationship, Ryan was the stay-at-home parent while I worked, which made him the primary parent. I didn't know how the courts would see that in terms of custody, like, "Yeah, he's horrible to you but what has he done to your children?"

On some level, I knew too much about the law to trust it with this decision. And if, God forbid, they saw it that way and I was out of the equation, what would he do to the kids when his punching bag (me) wasn't around?

Like so many other abusees, I was trapped. By my circumstances and by my fears in changing them.

To cap it all off was the shame. If I went public with what had been happening, it would have made it into my place of work. My colleagues would know. The judge would know. Everyone would find out that I had made the poorest choice in one of the biggest human decisions out there: who to take as our partner.

It is clear to me now that shame was probably the biggest inhibitor for me on this list. Don't make it yours.

And if you want to enroll in this course or work with me in any way to move forward with your life, go to www.beatrizpelayogarcia.com/course/.

I'd love to listen and see how I can help you.

Stories From my Ministry

"I see human beings at tough points

in their life and work to see them

into a better, elevated future.

Into future 'present moments'

that are not lived with breath held."

I see my law firm, Distinguished Legal, almost as my ministry. It is where I live my mission, my mission to help. To help people in need. I don't do this as a hobby, and I don't do this for the money. I do this as a calling. People have written to me and told me that, "Beatríz, you are my escape plan." That makes me feel good. That makes me feel like I am doing my job, like I am living my mission.

There is a range of abuse and domestic violence cases that come through my doors and into my office. While they are not fun, it is what I signed up for. My dream from a young age was to become a lawyer and to help people with both my knowledge and my compassion. Hopefully I bring some wisdom into the job with me as well. I worked hard when I was young to go to excel in law school while working full time. I prepared for the Bar more than anyone I have ever met. I have been running a successful practice for a long time. My clients come in with a problem and I do whatever I can to help. My main aim is to listen, to listen and then to employ my experience and expertise with the law to help.

I also bring my own personal experience into the fray, helping my clients in both elite-level attorney and elite-level human-experience ways. I try to help my clients onto a path of healing and a path of moving on, of moving forward. I talk about the polaroid verses the entire film. I talk about escape plans. I talk about making the decisions that prioritize real living over mere survival. I talk about a lot of the things I am putting down in this book, and talk about a lot of things I haven't put down in this book.

My work is my passion. I am a lot better mother these past few years, yes, but it has not detracted from my commitment to my profession. I am an attorney. I am here to help. I am here in service.

I see human beings at tough points in their life and work to see them into a better, elevated future. Into future 'present moments' that are not lived with breath held.

I work comprehensively with my clients. Many become my friends. I am there for them as both their lawyer and as a sort of psychologist and life-coach. I am there for them, however I can be. If you're reading this and are looking to talk with someone, go to my website at www.beatrizpelayogarcia.com and shoot me an email. While part of me hopes to never have to speak with someone professionally, another part really does.

At this point, I'll take a break from my life and my thoughts to lightly detail three cases that have been okayed by clients to go into this book. Still, I'll change the names and glaze over many of the details.

One client I'll refer to here as Violet, like me—and like a lot of us—just never knew what she would be coming home to. Never knew how her partner (and abuser) was going to act on a certain night.

The incident that led her to come to our firm for support occurred when she and her children arrived back at their home after a day out, only to find it in shambles. Stuff everywhere, things broken, the place disheveled. Violet initially thought it may have been an unknown intruder, but when the police found no evidence of forceful entry, she knew it had to have been her husband. It wasn't the first time he'd done something like this.

He'd also had his moments of rampage against Violet, calling her the standard but awful names of "bitch" and "whore," no matter if it was alone or with the children present. They'd often hear everything he said.

And, like many abusers, it was often the simplest of things that could set him off. One time it was that he couldn't find the house phone, the cordless landline, and he accused Violet of taking it. She hadn't. His voice was loud, and he was livid. The children, we were told, were scared, pale, and shaking. One of the children was so frightened that he urinated his pants.

After the break-in by her husband, Violet was encouraged by the police to grab some necessities and "go somewhere safe."

Like most of the clients we see, this was not the first time but the last straw. And in our consults and meetings, the rest of the story came out: Once when she was confused about where a new bike rack had come from, she asked her husband about it. He didn't respond with words so much as by dropping the apparatus on her. It was obviously very heavy, very hard and sharp, and it left her injured.

Once, when he'd accused her of taking his cellphone, he ran after her, threateningly so, caught up to her in the doorway, and slammed the door on her leg, causing injury.

Not even Christmas morning was sacred. Violet had gone to her parent's home to open presents with her children. Her husband had chosen not to participate, opting to stay at home by himself. When Violet and the children returned home, they found something odd—nearly every framed photograph of them or the family was turned around to face the wall or in the trash.

It was not a healthy relationship. And after that final straw with the ramshackled house, Violet called us—and our firm assisted her in filing a restraining order and worked to ultimately grant her temporary legal custody and full physical custody of her children.

The children's father did receive day visits on alternate weekends as well as a weekly visit for a midweek dinner.

An additional outcome provided for the children to attend individual and conjoint therapy so they might begin the healing process.

Going forth, communications were monitored by a resource called Our Family Wizard, which allows for counsel and the courts to review true communications without any omissions or fabrications from the parties involved.

We helped, and Violet and her children are now living a happier life.

Another client who has given us the go ahead to speak about her story is someone we will call Tiffany. The father of her children had been making threats against her and her boyfriend for nearly an entire year, going as far as to saying remarks about "wanting her to die." When he found out Tiffany's current address—where she and her children and her new partner were living—she became fearful and came to our firm.

We helped in every way that we could.

We quickly learned the extent of the abuse within her relationship to the children's father: a classic and tragic history of abuse. Their relationship had been plagued by the physical, verbal, and emotional abuse that haunts many of our clients. After Tiffany gathered the courage to leave him, to find her escape plan and follow through on getting out, she moved in with her sister. Like we all should, she knew she had that safe place to go.

However, the father of the children found out where she was and knew the house; he would soon be found sitting outside of the home, simply waiting for Tiffany to come outside, and he would follow her to work. It felt menacing to our client.

Despite the separation, she did allow for regular visitations with the children. But the abuser used this to his advantage—claiming via text message during visitations that there was an emergency. This would get Tiffany to go to them where he would proceed to make disparaging remarks to her in front of the children. He would also send texts, of the nature that wished her to die, to say she would be better off dead.

His anger was not solely manifested against Tiffany; it was sometimes transferred to the children, as documented by his daughter's toe being smashed by him with a slammed bathroom door.

More so, he threatened to "snap and end it all" if she ever started seeing someone else, going even further by threatening to kill her new significant other if she brought him around the children.

When he learned their new address, Tiffany made the decision to call our firm. She was scared, and we helped. We listened to the story, used our experience and expertise, and were able to obtain a restraining order against her abuser while securing full legal and physical custody to Tiffany until he completed a court ordered batterer's intervention program.

Tiffany was able to live a little easier, and we were elated to be an advocate for her freedom.

Like I may have said, I have been doing this type of work in different capacities for decades. The clients we've helped are in the hundreds. Most I cannot share. But the final client story from my firm I'll detail here is from someone I'll call Monica. Her abuser at the time had threatened to kill her. He threatened not only to "blow her head off" but also threatened to kill their son, as well. He had a record for assault; he had put his hands on both Monica and their son, and she believed he was capable of following through on his threat.

It came to the point where Monica became afraid to leave him and their son alone because he was often neglectful and there were instances of physical harm. He had also smacked Monica across both the face and the chest with his open palm. Some beatings were worse. The son witnessed to these violent outbursts.

After Monica came to see us, we did what we do, we helped—and she is now out of state with a TRO in place.

Nuggets from my Ten Love Letters Lesson in the Non-Toxic Forgiveness Course

"We are our thoughts.

If we think we can or think we can't,

the answer is yes."

In addition to my work with Distinguished Legal, I have mentioned how I also work with victims of abuse solely in the healing realm. I'll return here to give a glimpse of this work.

I talk a lot about the Escape Plan.

When suffering within an abusive relationship, you must know that an escape plan is coming. This is an invitation to shift in mindset. The hardest thing thus far has been in holding on and not seeing a way out. In treading water and not seeing the shore. In sinking and just trying to survive.

To escape, we need a shift to take place, a shift in mindset. A shift in knowing. This is the first step.

Even admitting, "Though I don't know how, I will get out of this" is a good place to start. When you come to the realization that you have to get out, the escape plan will come. Trust me on this one.

Until I embraced the mindset that 'even though I don't know how I will do it but I know I will do it,' I was trapped. Once I shifted my mindset to 'I got this'—I know I will do this and I will discover the how—I knew the escape plan was coming.

Endeavor to put your mind into a state of ease and the escape will come. Accept that even if you don't know how, you will.

Embracing the unknown is powerful. Take the fork in the road and go.

*

No one is going to judge you harder than you judge yourself. No one. Don't give yourself shame. Don't give yourself a hard time. People will give you support and love. One thing I tell people all the time is that "there is support and love on the other side of this."

We are all our own harshest judge. Others will see us with light in their eyes. They will. And these people are out there.

To help me on my journey, I began saying this mantra: "When would now be a good time to change my life(?)" It is both a question and a directive. The answer is directed-to right in the question—and that answer is 'Now.'

You can't fight with it. You can't even argue with it. The answer is right there: Now.

These words work with all kinds of decisions.

When would now be a good time to clean out my closet? Now. When would now be a good time to go to the gym? Now. When would now be a good time to escape this abuse, this terror?

Now.

Also, endeavor to internalize that: More people love you than you ever thought possible. There is so much love waiting for you. You are not alone. So many people, more than you ever thought possible, are going to come out and show up for you. Go find them. Let them find you. Receive them, receive their words and receive their understanding and receive their love.

We must do this because one thing that abusers know how to do is to isolate their victims from those they love. It's tactical. An abuser's aim is to get you cornered, to get you feeling 'left alone,' to cut you off from your friends and family. You may even be questioning, "How do I go ask for help from people I haven't interacted with in a long time?"

Answer: You can. Answer: You will, because you have to.

It's your life—and even if you've been cut off from these people for some time, they love you. They will help.

I had to reconnect with someone, for example, who's wedding I missed because I had too many bruises on my body. No text or nothing, I just didn't show up, felt like I couldn't show up. Was it difficult to pick up the phone a few months later and call her? Yes, it was. But it was doable, and it had to be done. So I did.

Pick up the phone. Make the call.

*

I like this little quote, and it goes, "Choose Yourself, and Choose Life."

To achieve it, we must first choose ourselves—no one else is going to do that for us. If you are living in an abusive relationship, you are not really living but merely trying to survive. I know I was. And it is no state within which to exist.

Choose to live! This life is meant to be more than a constant state of survival. It took me a long time, but I finally did. And it's beautiful. It's wonderful—it's alive and fun, giggles with the girls and hugs with my boys. It is living.

Once we choose ourselves, once we elevate ourselves, we have instantly chosen life. Try it. Choose yourself and see where it leads.

We owe it to ourselves to do this. Because the longer we stay in a state of trauma, the more damage it does. Psychological torments can manifest in your body. When you continue to endure the mental and spiritual anguish, it takes a toll on your body. For me it was irregular heartbeats. I was in and out of the hospital. People passed it off as, "oh, you have a stressful job." Nope. I loved (still do) being an attorney. My stress came from my home life. I had two lives: my work life and my home life. My work life was fun, dynamic, rewarding, good. My home life was the exact opposite. My home life, my abusive life at home, was what was putting me in the hospital due to my body manifesting the psychological (and physical) abuses.

And once we 'choose ourselves and choose life,' the forgiveness comes. We must all forgive ourselves. So say it with me, "I. Will. Forgive. Myself."

Even after I left, I was still judging myself, so harshly. I would literally ask myself a dozen times a day, "How could I have let myself get into this?"

It wasn't until I forgave myself that I was finally and truly free.

I had to escape, yes. I had to leave, yes. But before I forgave myself, I was still trapped. Trapped by my past. It was forgiveness—pure and complete self-forgiveness—that gave me the key to freedom.

You are not this experience; your abusive relationship is merely a blip in the Matrix.

I'll reiterate the analogy that our life is a movie, and this period of time is just a polaroid snap shot. And I encourage the people I work with not to focus on the picture, but upon the entire film. The credits haven't rolled yet. Heck, the entire second half of the film—when things really get good, and the protagonist (You!) overcomes all the obstacles to arrive at the happy ending—hasn't screened yet.

Stop looking at the polaroid of your life and start gleaning the entire motion picture of your life.

*

My definition of Non-Toxic Forgiveness is, simply, to 'forgive from a place of ownership.'

Seems easy enough, but it can take time. What I mean by forgiving from a place of ownership is to say: "I made these decisions, they were a part of me, and I forgive that within me which made them. I take 100% extreme ownership of my past choices, and that gives me empowered forgiveness. And empowered forgiveness gives me the lightness I need to thrive."

To help get here, I encourage you to really think about the words you say. There is a time and a place for 'victim language,' and there is a time in your journey to stop using it.

And with empowered forgiveness, we give ourselves the right, the privilege, to author our own lives, positively and with forward-progress. The words we say out loud and even the words we think in our head are absorbed right back into our being. They are. Positive mantras are found across the religious and spiritual spectrum for good reason.

It's not about, 'I don't have enough.' No, the universe will hear that and manifest that for you. It's about abundant thinking, about words of abundance coming out of your mouth and into the world.

We are our thoughts. If we think we can or think we can't, the answer is yes. The ability to think 'we can' starts with awareness. It starts with being aware of the thoughts we are thinking, the words we are saying, and the emotions we are experiencing.

Awareness is always the first step. Awareness leads to perspective, the perspective to say: "If I were someone else looking in, what would I see?"

We see others so clearly. Can see exactly what is going on with their relationships and how they treat themselves. With ourselves, though it seems like it should be easier, it just plain is not.

Awareness leads to forgiveness. Forgiveness leads to release. Release leads to freedom. Freedom leads to a positive and happy life.

You deserve this. Know it.

A Brief Review—and Father's Day

"Your escape plan

is

coming."

Walking away from this story, if nothing else, I encourage you to retain the following concepts, to internalize some of the ideas we have spoken about, and to hold onto them as you walk toward a freer self.

The hardest thing about an abusive relationship is getting out. Knowing how to get out. You may be feeling completely powerless, but you can do it. You have power. You have the power. Be ready. The escape plan is coming. The escape is already manifesting. Make it come true.

No one will ever judge you harder than you have judged yourself. Talk to people. Open up. Go to meetings. Talk with yourself. Try to find some stillness, and the healing will come.

More people love you, and will love you, than you ever thought possible.

Choose yourself and choose life.

Forgive yourself.

You are not this experience.

Your best life is possible. Why? Because you say so.

When would 'Now' be a good time to change your life?

The answer is right now. The longer we put it off—whether it is existing in an abusive relationship or for some other change we must implement to live a happy life—the more difficult it becomes.

For me it was always, "When I don't know, I just don't know," and then, one day, it changed to the understanding that, "I have control of right now."

If we put things off to the future, they remain there. The rainbow will never be reached. It stays in the distance, never reachable.

The now, the present, is what we can control. Yesterday is gone, tomorrow is unknown, and today is what we have. All of life is a series of todays, a series of right nows. Every second of every day, it is 'right now.' So, we should make our 'right nows' count. Because, when we do, it makes the ensuing 'right nows' so much better.

There is a cumulative power to living in the moment. It makes the next moment, which has already become 'the moment,' better.

And watch out for paralysis by analysis. Too much thought can be our worst enemy. It was for me. It keeps us from feeling, keeps us from listening to our instincts. Too much thinking prevents action.

The situation is here. Now it becomes a matter of, "how can change I change it for the better?"

I can honestly say, in this 'right now' of my life, I am a happy person. It started a few years ago, when the weight (both physical and metaphoric) had finally been shed and I said to myself, "I am ready to date."

Because that meant that I finally loved myself again. I loved myself enough to try and go give love to someone else.

I was no longer, for any reason, ashamed. I had escaped Ryan. I had become the mother I always wanted to be. I had shed 200 pounds of addictive behavior.

It happened when I learned to stop forgiving toxically and start forgiving healthily.

Back before I learned to love myself again and was still mired in my relationship to the father of my children, I used to carry insane amounts of cash and my passport wherever I went. Because I was afraid. Afraid of what may come next, afraid of having to get out. But I never followed through on it. That passport and all that cash was for an escape plan that never hatched.

In this 'right now' of my life, I still carry a passport and a fair amount of money on me. But it's not for escape; it's for adventure. Now it's for road trips, for spontaneous excursion with Conrad and Joshua. It's for fun. I carry those things around me, now, not for fear but for happiness.

I still always have my packed bag ready to go. But not to escape, rather to have fun hanging out with my kids.

"Conrad," I'll say, "pack your bag! Mom's gonna be home in an hour and we're going somewhere!"

And we go. Off into the horizon. It sometimes feels like a fairytale.

And when we return, my sons have a new father figure in their life. A good one. The best. My father. Their *abuelo*.

It's not all that uncommon among Latino families for *niños* to spend a lot of time with their grandparents. It's a cultural practice that goes back a long time. It offers a lot of unity, a lot of strength, to unite three generations—the learning that goes on, the wisdoms and laughter (and delicious food) that get exchanged and absorbed.

Joshua and Conrad (Conrad especially) stay the night over at grandparent's house often. Just watching movies and hanging out. Just 'being' with family that shows them love. Sometimes I'm there with them, and sometimes I'll drop them off so they can enjoy their company without mom around.

(I think they get more sweets that way.)

After a few years, Ryan did get some of his visitation rights back. They are few and far between but he still, on some level, gets to spend time with the children.

"Any day but Father's Day," I told him. "That day will no longer be tarnished."

See, that's because Father's Day is for good things. Father's Day is for positive male influence in my son's lives. Father's Day is for fishing trips with their grandfather. Father's Day is for happiness.

Father's Day is for my boys and their *abuelo*.

Anger or Forgiveness?

"We can free ourselves whenever

we are ready.

We hold the key—and it is found

between our ears and in that beating

muscle in our chest."

The way I see healthy forgiveness is as an ongoing journey. It's not 'one and done.' When I see myself acting a certain way, when I'm projecting my level of distrust into someone I'm dating, for example, I stop myself. I halt.

Because when we don't forgive, when we hold a grudge in spite, as my mom says, "it's like drinking poison and expecting someone else to die."

So I stop, I W.A.I.T., and I let go. And I forgive again.

It's almost like a drug addict (well, any addict) and their addictions. It may get easier to not put that needle in your arm, but the desire is, on some level, always there.

To overcome this, I now tell myself that, "I get to forgive. I get to forgive—again." Just like with sin in the Catholic Church; there's not always a new transgression; a lot of the time we must simply repent, again and again, for past actions. For past situations. For past experiences.

And so I forgive over and over. Most of my forgiveness, the forgiveness I need to keep giving, is still for myself. I still wake up in the middle of the night and cannot believe the decisions I made in the past, the decisions I made as a younger person. I still cannot believe what those decisions put my sons through. I still cannot believe I didn't leave after that first time he struck me in the face outside the bar.

So, yeah, I'm still a work in progress. My relationship with myself is still a work in progress. Always will be. While I am better, better than I was before, I can still be better, more in flow, more open and sharing and forgiving.

Not toxically, mind you. Healthily.

And we forgive in proportion to our consciousness. At first, I forgave because of what my mom told me—that harboring unforgiveness is like drinking the poison and expecting the other person to suffer. I saw the logic in her words, and so I heeded them. But it was still a little outside-in. Still a little like I was doing something because I was 'supposed to.'

Now I look at healthy forgiveness as opportunity, as something that fills up my soul. "I get to forgive!" is how I voice this act now.

I used to treat forgiveness like a barter, like, "If I give this, then I'll get that." It was so transactional.

Healthy forgiveness for myself and for others, now, comes from a place of joy. It comes from a place of spirit. And it gives me complete agency within the situation. It gives power—good, healthy power—when we forgive.

Conversely, if I didn't healthily forgive Ryan, for example, he would still hold power over me. He doesn't anymore. If I did not forgive myself for past decisions, then my fear would still hold power over me. It does not anymore.

To me, forgiveness is a pathway to reclaiming my power and standing in it. I feel that forgiveness can be that for you as well.

Because forgiveness makes us lighter. It helps us drop the weight and float through life without stress and with a smile on our face. Some of us manifest forgiveness a little differently: A friend of mine used to literally wish death upon her co-parent. They did not have a healthy relationship, and that's how she felt about him. But she needed to change her mindset toward it. She did it her own way. She came to hold a picture of him on her altar, just so she could look at him and, as she told me, "see him as a child." To see his decisions and his being as something childlike, something that she could envision and see and then forgive.

That was the way she chose to regain her power. We can all do it differently. Just make sure it is healthy, for you.

For me, it was always like, "what created this in Ryan?" At some point, something had to have happened to him for him to become 'him.' I strove to come up with a formula for why he ended up this way. I was always trying to intellectualize why he was him and why I fell in love with it.

It wasn't a healthy way to look at it, I came to see, so I don't do that anymore. "It was what it was;" that's how I look at it now. It happened. Move on.

I don't let my anger at myself and at Ryan hold me down anymore. In this 'right now' of my life, I see my past as wings. Wings upon which I am flying. If I hadn't have had to overcome what I've overcome, I wouldn't be flying as high.

I am living the joy of my sorrow unmasked.

I love myself—I love myself right now, for all I am—and I wouldn't be me without what I went through. I wouldn't be as strong. I wouldn't be as balanced. I'd probably still be buying PlayStations to show my love to my children. Maybe I'd still be 350 pounds.

I had to go through it all to have arrived where I've arrived.

Only I haven't arrived yet. None of us have because the journey is the destination. And I walk the journey of forgiveness and love. And I still have half my life to keep walking the path.

You do, too.

True forgiveness allowed me to wake up in the morning with peace in my heart. True forgiveness allowed me to regain the power of how I live my life. True forgiveness allowed me to become the best mother I could be. True forgiveness allowed me to write this book. True forgiveness allowed me to find myself. True forgiveness allowed me to find, to discover, to rediscover, Love.

And true forgiveness is the expansion of heart. Jesus teaches a lot of people about this. About forgiveness as the release of weight, of forgiveness as a path to physical healing and emotional transcendence.

And the opposite of forgiveness, Jesus or Muhammad or Gandhi may teach us, is anger. Because anger is self-imposed shackles.

Alas, the decision between forgiveness and anger is all up to us. We are given a situation and it is our actions—within our mind, through our thoughts, with our feelings— that selects which fork in the road we will travel upon.

Forgiveness or anger? Anger or forgiveness?

"Shit happens," someone once told me. "But suffering is optional."

It's all in our mind. We can free ourselves whenever we are ready. We hold the key—and it is found between our ears and in that beating muscle in our chest.

Fear, and Overcoming It

"Life can be lived without fear dictating what we do. Life can be lived free."

That time with the wire hanger.

Stabbed, bloody, terrified, I got out of the house. I no wallet or keys and I couldn't find any shoes. He'd hid all that from me, per usual. Barefoot, I went outside to throw away a dirty diaper because Ryan told me to do it, saying I was "shit and so you have to throw out the shit!"

But—when I walked outside and looked back to the door, he was not there, wasn't there staring at me, wasn't there watching me like he always was.

So I ran. I didn't think. I just ran.

And ran.

I ran to the local strip mall. I called 9-1-1. Not for the police, not to report what had just happened to me, not to make sure Ryan ended up in jail—no, not that, just to get the medical attention for myself so I wouldn't die.

I made the call and waited, bleeding steadily out onto the pavement. I had no shelter nor car, I just stood close to the payphone, as if standing in the proximity of something tall and stable would somehow make me less exposed. And, too, in case I began to feint from blood loss and needed to hold onto something. I finally heard the sirens, and then I saw the ambulance. The paramedics leapt out of the vehicle and ran to me.

They fired off questions at me, questions I deflected.

"Just take me to the hospital," I said.

They kept asking me questions. "What happened?" they said. "Why are you bleeding?"

"I was hit."

"Beatríz, who did this to you?"

"I was hit," I said, looking to the ground. "Just give me treatment."

I was being evasive beyond belief, and the paramedics did what they could to stop the bleeding. They checked my vitals and performed a series of field-tests and loaded me up into the ambulance and took me to the hospital.

The police arrived shortly after. In the white staleness of the room, all those beeping machines and medical personnel rushing in and out, they, too, asked me questions. Lots of them. They had out their pens and pads of paper, looking to write down what I would tell them. I still wouldn't give a straight answer.

"You know you can go to jail for not cooperating with our investigation?"

"Throw the book at me," I said.

I simply did not care. In that moment I just wanted to not die. I just wanted my children to be safe. My mind was a frozen-up blur, my most toxic relationship, the one with myself, rearing its ugly and misguided head.

Then I stopped.

I started breathing intentionally. I took a step back in my mind. I gained some much-needed clarity. Some much-needed clarity about the situation. Some much-needed clarity about the last three years of my life. Some much-needed clarity on the relationship I had with my children. Some much-needed clarity on the relationship I had with myself.

I picked up the hospital phone and called my mom.

She picked up. "What's going on, Beanny?"

I finally told her.

"*Ay Dios mío*," she said in a whisper. "My God."

"I know, mom. I'm sorry."

"No, you don't be sorry. You be thankful you are alive. You be thankful Joshua and Conrad are alive."

I knew my parents were about to leave on a vacation. "I just wanted to tell you. You go enjoy your trip, mom. We'll talk more when you get back."

"Beatríz! There is no way we are going anywhere. We are going to stay here and get you home, to our house, to the home you grew up in. Where you will be safe."

"No, go on your vacation."

"Mija, we're coming to get you."

"If you don't go—if I cause you to miss your vacation—I'll never tell you anything again."

"Mija, don't say that. Father and I will get your room ready for you. I'll send your sister to pick you up."

"Okay," I said.

"We are here for you, Beatríz."

"Thank you. Oh—and mom?"

"Yes?"

"Have her bring me some shoes."

*

My sister picked me up from the hospital and drove me to my parent's house. And then she went to pick up my sons.

But why didn't I tell anything to the police about Ryan? About him stabbing me with wire blades, about him cutting and gouging and almost killing me?

Fear. It was because of fear. It was because of that image, burned in my mind, of Ryan killing me and then killing the kids and then killing himself in his 'blaze of glory.'

Fear—it truly can paralyze us. If you are in an abusive relationship or know someone who is, please see this fear for what it is. Identify it. Overcome it.

I did. You can too. You must. Life can be lived without fear dictating what we do. Life can be lived free. Life can be lived happy.

On Forgiveness

"The river running dry in autumn forgives the rains for not falling because it knows the snow will soon come."

Forgiveness is, perhaps, the most elevated of human characteristics we can offer in our lives—or is it the most basic, the most primal?

You see, forgiveness is found throughout nature—"hey, you interrupted my drink at the watering hole, but I've had my time and I suppose I'll forgive you and let you have yours."

The river running dry in autumn forgives the rains for not falling because it knows the snow will soon come.

We humans do this, too; we must often forgive the current moment for not being perfect because of an understanding that everything is a circle.

The renown German philosopher, Frederick Nietzsche said it like this: "All that is straight lies. All truth is crooked. Time itself is a circle." (He also said something like: it is not a lack of love that makes unhappy marriages, but a lack of friendship.)

Back to forgiveness. When I made the conscious decision to lose the weight I'd gained, on some level, I had to seek forgiveness from it for not feeding it what it had grown used to. My body, too, on some level, had to forgive me for not giving it what it had grown used to.

And ultimately, my body had to forgive me for making it double in size in the first place. I had to forgive myself for this. I had to forgive before I could move forward.

Forgiveness lies at the core of Christianity (forgive 70x7, etc.) and at the core of many other belief systems. It lay at the core of familial and marital love. It lay at the core of the successful relationship. Forgiveness lay at the core of so much of what we humans do on this earth because, we, as it were, make mistakes. To error is human, right?

We are far from perfect. We all know this about ourselves (or we should!) and so we acknowledge that others are not perfect either.

At some point or another, we will all be assholes. We will all act rash or foolhardy. We will all blunder and error.

If you still have friends in your life, then you have forgiven. If you still love your family members, then you have forgiven. If you still love your dog or your cat, then you have forgiven.

The thing is, some forgiveness is more difficult to give. It is easy to forgive a child for the white lie they told to get their hands into or out of the cookie jar. It is much more difficult to forgive an adult who lies to you to get their hands into or out of the cookie jar. It is harder still when a spouse breaks the soul contract between you and begins to hurt you intentionally. And then continues to do it—to stab you and knife you and use your kids as ultimate-bait to keep you feeling trapped so he can do it all over again tomorrow.

Some people would look at what Ryan did to me and what other abusers have done to countless abusees as unforgiveable. Maybe it is. We all have the right to see things our own way. All I can do is speak from my experience, speak for what helped me move on and move forward.

When the time was right—when I'd cursed enough and cried enough and processed enough—I had to forgive my abuser to release the weight and stop feeling controlled by the past. Then I had to work on forgiving myself.

*

Even if there is no abuse, relationships between human beings are hard. We are not cows; we are not ants; we are complex beings with complex thought-systems that lead to complex circumstances. We can deceive. We can do bad things to get what we want. But we can, all of us, also be beautiful.

We are all wired a little bit differently. If there are eight-billion people on the planet, then there are eight-billion ways to see something.

And men and woman? Yeah, we are a little bit from Mars and Venus, respectively. If we enter into a relationship with someone, there should be some level of understanding of this and some level of commitment to overcoming this. Our differences can be a barrier, for sure, but puzzle pieces without differences cannot interlock.

And when our union leads to birth, to child, to children, the soul contract had better be pretty strong. Mine was not. Mine was broken.

I've non-toxically forgiven myself for that.

I am now actively dating and even perhaps open to finding another person to be with long term. I finally trust myself to make this decision—because I forgave my past decisions and have empowered my present and future decisions. With tons of time in therapy and tons of time in self-love and self-help, I know I am journeying in a place where I am making conscious decisions that lead to conscious actions.

If you have previously been in a tough relationship, know there is someone out there who will love you for exactly who you are. And know that when you forgive and love yourself, this person will be universally attracted to you.

Life is not easy. Forgiveness, in my opinion, makes it a little easier.

Life is Good

Some last words of advice, some last words of encouragement, and then I'll say goodbye.

The first is: be the aberration, not the norm.

In a society that many of us recognize as a bit messed up, being abnormal can be a good thing. Moving backward from a backward moving mechanism can move us forward.

If you see someone being abused, if you hear screams from your neighbor's house, tell someone. Be different and do something about it. Pick up the phone. Be human. Have a heart. Help. Especially if there are children involved.

I wish someone would have with me. I know people heard things. I know people suspected things. But they stayed silent. Everyone stayed silent. I'm not placing blame; I know it was my own inaction which led my children to have the memories they have, but we can all extend our hand. We can all trust our instincts and act.

Silence can literally equal death. Speak up.

And if you know someone in an abusive relationship, tell them simply: "When you are ready, you have a spot to land."

Abuse is all-to common in our society. We can all help to alleviate it. We can all help. We can, and we should.

*

Years ago, Joshua came up to me with a question. "Mom," he said, a look of confusion upon his face, "I see the wire hanger—I see dad and you and a wire hanger... is this real or did I make it up in my head?"

I almost began to cry but I took a breath and calmed my soul. I told him, "Yes, that memory is real."

My boys and I have worked uncountable hours in therapy and on our road trips and in our home to navigate the memories they have, both the conscious and the subconscious ones. Most of their memories are not visible but audible, memories of me screaming in the living room when they were in their bedrooms. And some are still very vivid.

My children never saw me being stabbed. Thank God for that. They never saw me being pushed down the staircase or having a pillow shoved into my face as the breath left my lungs.

But Joshua does remember the wire hanger, the weapon that sent me to the hospital, the trauma that finally pushed me to tell my mom what was going on and ultimately led to me complete my escape plan.

So what do I tell Joshua?

I tell him that it happened. I tell him that it is in the past. I tell him that we have awakened from a nightmare so we may live our dream.

And that life is good.

www.ingramcontent.com/pod-product-compliance
Lightning Source LLC
Chambersburg PA
CBHW071432150426
43191CB00008B/1100